EAA Lecture Notes

Editors

H. Bühlmann   A. Pelsser
W. Schachermayer   H. Waters   D. Filipovic, Chair

EAA Lecture Notes is a series supported by the European Actuarial Academy (EAA GmbH), founded on the 29 August, 2005 in Cologne (Germany) by the Actuarial Associations of Austria, Germany, the Netherlands and Switzerland. EAA offers actuarial education including examination, permanent education for certified actuaries and consulting on actuarial education.

actuarial-academy.com

EAA Lecture Notes

Wüthrich, M.V.; Bühlmann, H.; Furrer, H. **Market-Consistent Actuarial Valuation** 2007

Mario Valentin Wüthrich · Hans Bühlmann ·
Hansjörg Furrer

Market-Consistent Actuarial Valuation

With 13 Figures and 17 Tables

 Springer

Authors

Mario Valentin Wüthrich

Department of Mathematics
ETH Zürich
CH-8092 Zürich
Switzerland
E-mail: mario.wuethrich@math.ethz.ch

Hans Bühlmann

Department of Mathematics
ETH Zürich
CH-8092 Zürich
Switzerland
E-mail: hbuhl@math.ethz.ch

Hansjörg Furrer

Swiss Life
General-Guisan-Quai 40
CH-8022 Zürich
Switzerland
E-mail: hansjoerg.furrer@swisslife.ch

Library of Congress Control Number: 2007931823

Mathematics Subject Classification (2000): 91B30, 91B28

ISSN 1865-2174

ISBN 978-3-540-73642-4 Springer Berlin Heidelberg New York

Springer is a part of Springer Science+Business Media GmbH
springer.com
© Springer-Verlag Berlin Heidelberg 2008

Typesetting: by the author and VTEX using a Springer LaTeX macro package
Cover design: *WMXDesign* GmbH, Heidelberg
Printed on acid-free paper   SPIN:151163   40/3180/VTEX   5 4 3 2 1 0

Preface

The balance sheet of an insurance company is often difficult to interprete. This derives from the fact that assets and liabilities are measured by different yardsticks. Assets are mostly valued at market prices; liabilities – as far as they relate to contractual obligations to the insured – are measured by established actuarial methods. Since, in general, there is no trading market for insurance policies, the question arises how these actuarial methods need to be changed to give values – as if these markets existed. The answer to this question is "Market-Consistent Actuarial Valuation". These lecture notes explain the logical mathematical framework that leads to market-consistent values for insurance liabilities.

In Chapter 1 we motivate the use of market-consistent values. Solvency requirements by regulators are one major reason for it.

Chapter 2 introduces stochastic discounting, which in a market-consistent actuarial valuation replaces discounting with the classical technical interest rate. In this chapter we introduce the notion of "Financial Variables", (which follow the laws of financial markets) and the notion of "Technical Variables", (which are purely depending on insurance events).

In Chapter 3 the concept of the "Valuation Portfolio" (VaPo) is introduced and explained in the life insurance context. The basic idea is not to calculate in monetary values but in units, which are appropriately chosen financial instruments. For life insurance products this choice is quite natural. The risk due to technical variables is included in the protected (against technical risk) VaPo, denoted by VaPo^{prot}.

Financial Risk is treated in Chapter 4. It derives from the fact that the actual investment portfolio of the insurance company differs from the VaPo^{prot}. Ways to control the financial risk are Margrabe Options and/or (additional) Risk Bearing Capital.

In Chapter 5 the notion of the Valuation Portfolio (VaPo) and the protected (against technical risk) Valuation Portfolio (VaPo^{prot}) is extended to the non-life insurance sector. The basic difference to life insurance derives from the fact that in property-casualty insurance the technical risk is much more important. The discussion of appropriate risk measures (in particular the quadratic prediction error) is therefore a central issue.

The final Chapter 6 contains selected topics. We mention only the treatment of the "Legal Quote" in life insurance.

These lecture notes stem from a course on Market-Consistent Actuarial Valuation, so far given twice at ETH Zürich, namely in 2004/05 by HB and HJF and in 2006 by MW and HJF. MW has greatly improved on the first version of these notes. But obviously also this version is not to be considered as final. For this reason we are grateful that the newly created EAA Lecture Notes series gives us the opportunity to share these notes with many friends and colleagues, whom we invite to participate in the process of discussions and further improvement of the present text as well as of further clarification of our way of understanding and modeling.

The authors wish to thank Professor Paul Embrechts for his interest and constant encouragement while they were working on this project. His support has been a great stimulus for us.

It is also a great honour for us that our text appears as the first volume of the newly founded EAA Lecture Notes series. We are greatful to Peter Diethelm, who as Managing Director has been the driving force in getting this series started.

Zürich,   *Mario Wüthrich*
May 2007   *Hans Bühlmann*
                                                           Hansjörg Furrer

Contents

1

Introduction

1.1 Three pillar approach

The recent years have shown that (financial) companies need to have a good management, a good business strategy, a good financial strength and a good risk management in order to survive. It is essential that the risks are known, specified and controlled by the management.

Especially in the past few years, we have observed several failures of financial companies (for example Barings Bank, HIH Insurance Australia, etc.). From 1996 until 2002 many companies had different difficulties about solvency and liquidity. As a consequence, supervision and politics have started several initiatives to analyze these problems and to improve qualitative and quantitative risk management within the companies (Basel II, Solvency 2 and local initiatives like the Swiss Solvency Test [SST06], for an overview we refer to Sandström [Sa06]).

Concerning insurance companies: The goal behind all these initiatives is to protect the policyholder (and the injured, respectively) from the consequences of an insolvency of an insurance company. Hence, in most cases it is not primarily the object of the regulator to avoid insolvencies of insurance companies, but given an insolvency of an insurance company, the regulator has to ensure that all liabilities are covered with assets and can be fulfilled in an appropriate way (this is not the shareholder's point of view).

One special project was carried out by the "London working group". The London working group has analyzed 21 cases of solvency problems (actual failures and 'near misses') in 17 European countries. Their findings can be found in the famous Sharma Report [Sha02]. The main lessons learned are:

- In most cases bad management was the source of the problem.
- Another central problem was that often head office had designed business strategies which were not adapted to local situations.

From this perspective, what can we really do?

Sharma says: "Capital is only the second strategy of defense in a company, the first is a good risk management".

Supervision has started several initiatives to strengthen the financial basis and to improve risk managment thinking within the companies. Most of the new approaches and requirements (e.g. Basel II, Solvency 2, Swiss Solvency Test [SST06]) are formulated in three pillars:

1. Pillar 1: Minimum financial requirements (quantitative requirements)

2. Pillar 2: Supervisory review process, adaquate risk management (qualitative requirements)

3. Pillar 3: Market discipline and public transparency

Consequences: Regulators as well as actuaries, mathematicians and risk managers in financial companies and universities search for new solvency guidelines. These guidelines should be **risk-adjusted**. Moreover they should be based on a **market-consistent valuation** of the balance sheet (full balance sheet approach).

From these perspectives we derive the valuation portfolio which reflects a market-consistent actuarial valuation of our balance sheet. Moreover, we describe the uncertainties within this portfolio which corresponds to a risk-adjusted analysis of our assets and liabilities.

1.2 Solvency

The International Association of Insurance Supervisiors IAIS [IAIS05] defines solvency as follows

"the ability of an insurer to meet its obligations (liabilities) under all contracts at any time. Due to the very nature of insurance business, it is impossible to guarantee solvency with certainty. In order to come to a practicable definition, it is necessary to make clear under which circumstances the appropriateness of the assets to cover claims is to be considered, ...".

Hence the aim of solvency is to protect the policyholder or injured, respectively. As it is formulated in Swiss law: it is not the main goal of the regulator to avoid bankruptcies of insurance companies, but in case of a bankruptcy the regulator tries to guarantee that the company is still able to meet its obligations. Avoiding bankruptcies must be the main task of the management and the board of an insurance company. A side effect of the aim of solvency is to ensure a certain stability of the financial market.

In this lecture we give a mathematical approach and interpretation to the solvency definition of the IAIS [IAIS05].

Let us start with two definitions:

1. **Available Solvency Surplus** (see [IAIS05]), or **Risk Bearing Capital** RBC (see [SST06]) is the difference between the value of the assets minus the value of the liabilities. This corresponds to the Available Risk Margin, the Available Risk Capacity or Financial Strength of a company.

2. **Required Solvency Margin** (see [IAIS05]) or **Target Capital** TC (see [SST06]) is the Required Risk Capital (from a regulatory point of view) in order to be able to run the business such that also certain adverse scenarios are covered (see solvency definition of the IAIS [IAIS05]). This is the Necessary Risk Capacity or Minimal Financial Requirement for writing certain business.

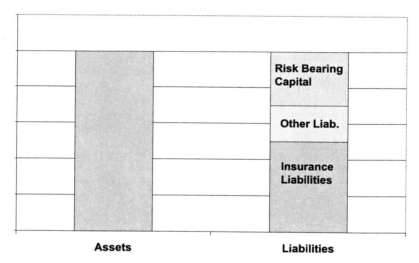

Fig. 1.1. Balance sheet of an insurance company

In general, supervision requires for a company to be solvent that

$$\text{TC} \overset{!!!}{\leq} \text{RBC.} \qquad (1.1)$$

Hence, given the amount of risk TC a company is exposed to, the regulators require that this risk is bounded by the available surplus RBC. That is, RBC defines the risk capacity of a company, which has to be compared to the required risk capacity TC.

Otherwise if (1.1) is not satisfied, the authorities force the company to do certain actions to improve the financial strength or to reduce the risks within the portfolio, such as: write less risky business, sell part of the business or even close the company, and make sure that another company guarantees the smooth runoff of the liabilities.

1.3 From the past to the future

A short overview on the historical developments of solvency requirements can be found in Sandström [Sa07].

In the past, the evaluation of the Risk Bearing Capital RBC was not based on a market-consistent valuation of assets and liablities (for example, insurance liabilities were measured by a statutorial approach which does not use market values). Moreover, the Target Capital TC was not defined risk-adjusted, for example, Solvency 1 Guidelines in non-life insurance were simply of the form

$$\text{Target Capital TC } = 16\% \text{ of premium}, \qquad (1.2)$$

and in life insurance they were of the form

$$\text{Target Capital TC } = 4\% \text{ of the mathematical reserves (financial risk)}$$
$$+3\text{‰ of capital at risk (technical risk).} \qquad (1.3)$$

These solvency rules are very simple and robust, easy to understand and to use. They are rule-based, but they are not risk-based, for example, the kind of business that is written does not matter and the differences between the asset and the liability profile are neglected.

Our goal in this lecture is to give a mathematical theory to a market-consistent valuation approach. Moreover, our model builds a bridge of understanding between actuaries and asset managers. In the past, actuaries were responsible for the liabilities in the balance sheet and asset manager were concerned with the active side of the balance sheet. But these two parties do not always speak the same language which makes it difficult to design a successful ALM strategy. In this lecture we introduce a language which allows actuaries and asset managers to communicate in a successful way which leads to a canonical risk-adjusted full balance sheet approach to the solvency problem.

1.4 Full balance sheet approach

A typical balance sheet of an insurance company contains the following positions:

Assets	Liabilities
bonds	claims reserves
stocks	mathematical reserves / reserves for annuities
real estate	unearned premium reserves
mortgages	bonus reserves
loans	bond issues
participations	derivative instruments
hedge funds	payables policyholder
private equity	payables agent
foreign exchange	payables reinsurance
receivables policyholder	pension fund employes
receivables agent	deferred expenses
deferred acquisition costs	taxes
receivables reinsurance	etc.
cash	
property	
deferred income	
etc.	

It is necessary that assets and liabilities are measured in a consistent way. Market values have no absolute significance, depending on the purpose other values may be better (for example statutorial values). But market values guarantee the switching property (at market price).

Applications of these lectures are found in:

- internal value based managment tools, dynamical financial analysis tools,
- internal risk management tools,
- for solvency purposes which are based on a market-consistent valuation,
- finding prices for trading insurance policies and for loss portfolio transfers.

As actuaries we have mostely been using deterministic models for discounting liabilities. As soon as interest rates become stochastic, life is much more complicated, for example, let $r > 0$ be a stochastic interest rate, then (by Jensen's inequality)

$$1 = E\left[\frac{1+r}{1+r}\right] \neq E\left[1+r\right] \cdot E\left[\frac{1}{1+r}\right] > 1, \qquad (1.4)$$

that is, in a stochastic environment we can not simply exchange the expectation of the stochastic return $1 + r$ with the expectation of the stochastic discount $(1+r)^{-1}$. This problem arises as soon as we work with random variables. In the next chapter we define a consistent model for discounting (deflation) cashflows.

1.5 Recent financial failures and difficulties

We close this chapter with some "bad" examples in the insurance industry. One should mention that the list is not complete, for example, it does not contain companies which were bought by other companies just before they would have collapsed.

- 1988-1991: Lloyd's London looses more than 3 billion USD due to asbestos and other health IBNR claims.
- 1993: Confederation Life Insurance, Canada, 1.3 billion USD is missing due to fatale errors in asset investments.
- 1997 Nissan Mutual Life, Japan, too high guarantees on rates cost 300 billion yen.
- 2000: Dai-ichi Mutual Fire and Marine Insurance Company, Japan, is liquidated, strategic mismanagement of their insurance merchandise.
- 2001: HIH Insurance Australia is liquidated since 4 billion USD are missing.
- 2001: Independent Insurance UK is liquidated due to rapid growth, insufficient reserves and not adequate premiums.
- 2001: Taisei Fire and Marine, Japan, missing 100 billion yen due to large reinsurance claims e.g. world trade center September 11, 2001.
- 2002 Gerling Global Re, Germany, seemed to be undercapitalized and underreserved for many years. Further problems arised by the acquisition of Constitution Re.
- 2003: Equitable Life Assurance Society UK is liquidated due to concentration and interest rate risks.
- 2003: KBV Krankenkasse, Switzerland, is liquidated due to financial losses caused by fraud.

2

Stochastic discounting

In this chapter we define a mathematically consistent model for calculating values of cash flows. The key objects are the so-called deflators which play the role of stochastic discount factors. Our definition (via deflators) leads to market values which are consistent with the usual financial theory that involves risk neutral valuation. Typically, in financial mathematics the pricing formulas are based on martingale theory (see, for example, Föllmer-Schied [FS04]), economists use the notion of state price density processes (see Malamud et al. [MTW07]) and actuaries use the terminology of deflators (see Duffie [Du96] and Bühlmann et al. [BDES98]). In this chapter we describe these terminologies.

2.1 Basic discrete time model

In this chapter we develop the theoretical foundations of market-consistent valuation.

We assume that we have a probability space $(\Omega, \mathcal{F}, P)$ and an increasing sequence of σ-fields $(\mathcal{F}_t)_{t=0,\ldots,n}$ with

$$\{\emptyset, \Omega\} = \mathcal{F}_0 \subset \mathcal{F}_1 \subset \ldots \subset \mathcal{F}_n \subset \mathcal{F}. \tag{2.1}$$

Moreover, assume that we have a sequence of $(\mathcal{F}_t)_{t=0,\ldots,n}$-adapted random variables

$$\mathbf{X} = (X_0, X_1, \ldots, X_n), \tag{2.2}$$

i.e. X_t is $\mathcal{F}_t$-measurable for all $t = 0, \ldots, n$. $\mathbf{X}$ is a (random) cash flow, with single payments X_t at time t. Our goal is to determine the value of such a cash flow $\mathbf{X}$ (see Figure 2.1).

We make some technical assumptions.

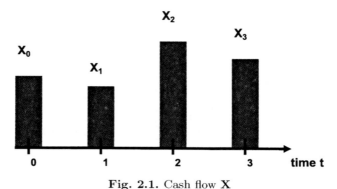

Fig. 2.1. Cash flow **X**

Assumption 2.1 *Assume that every coordinate of* **X** *is square integrable.*

This means that we assume that

$$\mathbf{X} = (X_0, X_1, \ldots, X_n) \in L^2_{n+1}(P), \tag{2.3}$$

where $L^2_{n+1}(P)$ is a Hilbert space with

$$E\left[\sum_{t=0}^{n} X_t^2\right] < \infty \qquad \text{for all } \mathbf{X} \in L^{n+1}(P), \tag{2.4}$$

$$< \mathbf{X}, \mathbf{Y} > = E\left[\sum_{t=0}^{n} X_t Y_t\right] \qquad \text{for all } \mathbf{X}, \mathbf{Y} \in L^2_{n+1}(P), \tag{2.5}$$

$$\|\mathbf{X}\| = < \mathbf{X}, \mathbf{X} >^{1/2} \qquad \text{for all } \mathbf{X} \in L^2_{n+1}(P). \tag{2.6}$$

Technical remark. The equality $\|\mathbf{X} - \mathbf{Y}\| = 0$ implies that $\mathbf{X} = \mathbf{Y}$, P-a.s. As usually done in Hilbert spaces, we identify random variables which are equal P-a.s.

Example 2.1 (Life insurance).

We consider a single policy. This policy creates several cash flows. On the one hand we have premiums Π_t coming in at time t, on the other hand there are expenses and benefits paid within the time interval $(t-1, t]$. If we map all cash flows inside $(t-1, t]$ to the end point of the time interval, we obtain a discrete cash flow for $t \in \mathbb{N}$:

$$X_t = -\Pi_t + \text{benefits and expenses paid within } (t-1, t]. \tag{2.7}$$

Henceforth, **X** denotes the cash flow generated by this single policy.

$\square$

Example 2.2 (Non-life insurance).

In non-life insurance the insurance company usually receives a (risk) premium at the beginning of a well-defined insurance period. Within this insurance period certain (well-defined, random) financial losses are covered. We denote this premium by $\Pi = -X_0$. If an event (claim) happens during that insurance period, several cash flows are generated to settle such a claim. That is, usually the insurance company can not immediately settle a claim. It takes quite some time until the ultimate claim is known. The delay in the settlement is due to the fact that, for example, it takes time until the total medical expenses are known, until the claim is settled at court, until the damaged building is fixed, until the recovery process is understood, etc.

Since one does not wait with the payments until the claim is finally settled (e.g. medical expenses and salaries are paid when they occur) a claim consists of several single payments X_t which reflect the on-going recovery process. Hence, the ultimate or total claim (nominal) is given by

$$C_n = \sum_{t=1}^{n} X_t, \tag{2.8}$$

where X_t $(t \leq n)$ denote the single payments and X_n denotes the final payment when the claim is closed/settled. The underwriting loss (nominal loss) can then be written as

$$UL = \sum_{t=0}^{n} X_t = -\Pi + C_n. \tag{2.9}$$

Remark. UL does not necessarily need to be negative to run successfully this non-life business. The nominal underwriting loss UL does not consider the financial income during the settlement of the claim. That is, the delay in the payments allows for discounting of the payments, i.e. generates investment incomes at the insurance company (see next sections).

$\square$

2.2 Market-consistent valuation in the basic discrete time model

We now want to value the (stochastic) cash flow $\mathbf{X}$. We proceed as in Bühlmann [Bü92] and [Bü95] using a positive continuous linear functional.

Definition 2.2

- $\mathbf{X} > 0 \Leftrightarrow X_k \geq 0$, *P-a.s., for all* $k = 0, \ldots, n$ *and there exists* $k \in \{0, \ldots, n\}$ *such that* $X_k > 0$ *with positive probability.*
- $\mathbf{X} \gg 0 \Leftrightarrow X_k > 0$ *P-a.s. for all* $k = 0, \ldots, n$.

Assumption 2.3 *Assume that $Q : L^2_{n+1}(P) \to \mathbb{R}$ is a positive, continuous, linear functional on $L^2_{n+1}(P)$.*

This means that the functional Q satisfies the following properties:

(1) Positivity: $\mathbf{X} > 0$ implies $Q[\mathbf{X}] > 0$.
(2) Continuity: For any sequence $\mathbf{X}^{(k)} \in L^2_{n+1}(P)$ with $\mathbf{X}^{(k)} \to \mathbf{X}$ in $L^2_{n+1}(P)$ as $k \to \infty$, we have $Q\left[\mathbf{X}^{(k)}\right] \to Q[\mathbf{X}]$.
(3) Linearity: For all $\mathbf{X}, \mathbf{Y} \in L^2_{n+1}(P)$ and $a, b \in \mathbb{R}$ we have

$$Q[a\mathbf{X} + b\mathbf{Y}] = a \cdot Q[\mathbf{X}] + b \cdot Q[\mathbf{Y}]. \qquad (2.10)$$

Terminology.
The map $\mathbf{X} \mapsto Q[\mathbf{X}]$ gives a monetary value $Q[\mathbf{X}] \in \mathbb{R}$ at time 0 to the cash flow $\mathbf{X}$. As we see below, this valuation will be done in a market-consistent way which leads to a risk neutral valuation scheme.

Remark. Assumptions (1) and (3) ensure that we do not have arbitrage (see Lemma 2.4 and Remark 2.7).

Lemma 2.3. *Assumptions (1) and (3) imply (2).*

Proof. Define $\mathbf{Y}^{(k)} = \mathbf{X}^{(k)} - \mathbf{X}$. Due to the linearity of Q it suffices to prove that $\mathbf{Y}^{(k)} \to 0$ in $L^2_{n+1}(P)$ implies that $Q\left[\mathbf{Y}^{(k)}\right] \to 0$.
In the first step we assume that $\mathbf{Y}^{(k)} > 0$. Then we claim

$$\mathbf{Y}^{(k)} \to 0 \text{ in } L^2_{n+1}(P) \text{ implies } Q\left[\mathbf{Y}^{(k)}\right] \to 0 \text{ as } k \to \infty. \qquad (2.11)$$

Assume (2.11) does not hold true, hence (using the positivity of the linear functional) there exists $\varepsilon > 0$ and an infinite subsequence k' of k such that for all k'

$$Q\left[\mathbf{Y}^{(k')}\right] \geq \varepsilon. \qquad (2.12)$$

Choose an infinite subsequence k'' of k' with

$$\sum_{k''} \left\|\mathbf{Y}^{(k'')}\right\| < \infty. \qquad (2.13)$$

We define

$$\mathbf{Y} = \sum_{k''} \mathbf{Y}^{(k'')}. \qquad (2.14)$$

Due to the completeness of $L^2_{n+1}(P)$ we know that $\mathbf{Y} \in L^2_{n+1}(P)$. But

$$Q[\mathbf{Y}] \geq Q\left[\sum_{k''=1}^{N} \mathbf{Y}^{(k'')}\right] \geq N \cdot \varepsilon \qquad \text{for every } N. \qquad (2.15)$$

This implies that $Q\left[\mathbf{Y}\right] = \infty$ is not finite, which is a contradiction.

Second step: Decompose $\mathbf{Y}^{(k)} = \mathbf{Y}_+^{(k)} - \mathbf{Y}_-^{(k)}$ into a positive and a negative part. Since $\|\mathbf{Y}_+^{(k)}\| \leq \|\mathbf{Y}^{(k)}\| \to 0$ and $\|\mathbf{Y}_-^{(k)}\| \leq \|\mathbf{Y}^{(k)}\| \to 0$ we see that

$$Q\left[\mathbf{Y}_+^{(k)}\right] \to 0 \text{ and } Q\left[\mathbf{Y}_-^{(k)}\right] \to 0. \tag{2.16}$$

Using once more the linearity of Q completes the proof.

□

Theorem 2.4 (Riesz representation theorem) *There exists $\varphi \in L_{n+1}^2(P)$ such that for all $\mathbf{X} \in L_{n+1}^2(P)$ we have*

$$Q\left[\mathbf{X}\right] = <\mathbf{X}, \varphi> = E\left[\sum_{t=0}^n X_t \cdot \varphi_t\right]. \tag{2.17}$$

Definition 2.5 *The vector φ (and its single components φ_t) is called deflator.*

The terminology deflator was introduced by Duffie [Du96] and Bühlmann et al. [BDES98]. In economic theory deflators are called state price densities.

Remarks. The deflator has the following properties:

- The positivity of Q ensures that $\varphi \gg 0$.
- φ_t may be chosen $\mathcal{F}_t$-adapted: Replace φ_t by $\widetilde{\varphi}_t = E\left[\varphi_t|\mathcal{F}_t\right]$. Then we have for all $\mathbf{X}$

$$Q[\mathbf{X}] = E\left[\sum_{t=0}^n X_t \cdot \varphi_t\right] = E\left[\sum_{t=0}^n X_t \cdot E\left[\varphi_t|\mathcal{F}_t\right]\right] = E\left[\sum_{t=0}^n X_t \cdot \widetilde{\varphi}_t\right]. \tag{2.18}$$

Hence, we may and will assume that φ_t is $\mathcal{F}_t$-adapted.
- There is exactly one $\mathcal{F}_t$-adapted φ (up to measure 0). Assume that there are two $\mathcal{F}_t$-adapted random variables φ and φ^* satisfying for all $\mathbf{X}$

$$Q\left[\mathbf{X}\right] = <\mathbf{X}, \varphi> = <\mathbf{X}, \varphi^*>. \tag{2.19}$$

But then

$$Q\left[\varphi\right] = \|\varphi\|^2 = <\varphi, \varphi^*>, \tag{2.20}$$
$$Q\left[\varphi^*\right] = <\varphi^*, \varphi> = \|\varphi^*\|^2. \tag{2.21}$$

This implies that

$$<\varphi^*, \varphi> = \|\varphi^*\| \cdot \|\varphi\|. \tag{2.22}$$

The Schwarz inequality says that φ and φ^* are equal up to a constant factor, P-a.s. But then the claim follows from (2.19).
- Furthermore, we assume that Q is such that $\varphi_0 \equiv 1$. This means that for a deterministic payment x_0 at time 0, we have $Q[(x_0, 0, \ldots, 0)] = x_0$. This means that at time 0 the functional Q delivers simply the nominal value.

2.2.1 Task of modelization

Find the appropriate Q or equivalently find the appropriate $\mathcal{F}_t$-adapted deflator φ!

The $\mathcal{F}_t$-adaptedness will be crucial in the sequel. It essentially means that the deflator φ_t (stochastic discount factor) is known at time t, and hence, allows for a direct connection of the $\mathcal{F}_t$-adapted cash flow X_t with the behaviour φ_t of the financial market at time t.

Examples of deflators/state price densities can be found in [Bü95], e.g. Ehrenfest Urn with limit Ornstein-Uhlenbeck model, or in Filipovic-Zabczyk [FZ02].

2.2.2 Understanding deflators

A **deflator** φ_t transports cash amount at time t to value at time 0. This transportation is a stochastic transportation. That is, a cash flow $\mathbf{X}_t = (0, \ldots, 0, X_t, 0, \ldots, 0)$ does not necessarily need to be independent of φ_t, i.e.

$$Q\left[\mathbf{X}_t\right] = E\left[X_t \cdot \varphi_t\right] \neq E\left[X_t\right] \cdot E\left[\varphi_t\right]. \tag{2.23}$$

We decompose the deflator φ_t into its **span-deflators**. Since $\varphi_t > 0$, P-a.s., we can build the following ratios for all $t > 0$, P-a.s.:

$$Y_t = \frac{\varphi_t}{\varphi_{t-1}}. \tag{2.24}$$

Hence $(Y_t)_t$ satisfies

$$\varphi_t = Y_1 \cdots Y_t = \prod_{k=1}^{t} Y_k. \tag{2.25}$$

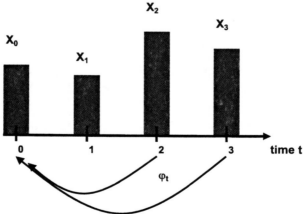

Fig. 2.2. Deflator φ and cash flow $\mathbf{X}$

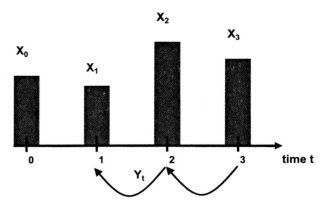

Fig. 2.3. Span-deflators Y_t and cash flow $\mathbf{X}$

Y_t is called span-deflator. Span deflators Y_t transport cash amount at time t to value at time $t - 1$.

Finally, we compare our deflators to the classical financial discounting. Denote by $\mathbf{Z}^{(t)} = (0, \dots, 0, 1, 0, \dots, 0)$ the cash flow of the **zero coupon bond** paying the amount 1 at time t. The value at time 0 of this zero coupon bond is given by

$$D_{0,t} = Q\left[\mathbf{Z}^{(t)}\right] = E\left[\varphi_t\right]. \tag{2.26}$$

$D_{0,t}$ denotes the value of the zero coupon bond $\mathbf{Z}^{(t)}$ at time 0. In financial literature $D_{0,t}$ is often denoted by $P(0, t)$, which is the value at time 0 of a contract paying 1 at time t.

Hence, also $D_{0,t}$ transports cash amount at time t to value in 0. But $D_{0,t}$ is $\mathcal{F}_0$-measurable, whereas φ_t is a $\mathcal{F}_t$-measurable random variable. This means that the deterministic discount factor $D_{0,t}$ is known at the beginning of the time period, whereas φ_t is only known at the end of the period $(0, t]$. As long as we deal with deterministic cash flows $\mathbf{X}$, we can work with either zero coupon bonds or deflators to determine the value at time 0. But as soon as the cash flows are probabilistic we need to work with deflators (see (2.23)) since X_t and φ_t may be influenced by the same factors (are dependent). An easy example is that X_t is an option that depends on the actual realization of φ_t. Various life insurance policy contain such financial options, that is, the insurance payout depends on the development of the financial market factors.

Classical **actuarial discounting** is taking a constant interest rate i. That is, in classical actuarial models φ_t has the following form

$$\varphi_t = (1 + i)^{-t}. \tag{2.27}$$

This definition would give a consistent theory but it is far from the economic observations in practice. This indicates that we have to be very careful with this deterministic model in a total balance sheet approach, since it implies that we obtain values far away from those consistent with the financial market values on the asset classes.

2.2.3 Toy example for deflators

In this subsection we give a toy example: In a first step we need a market model, which allows calibrating prices. In a second step we construct deflators (the example is taken from [Ja01]).

We consider a one-period model, and we assume that there are two possible states at time 1, namely $\{s_1, s_2\}$. For this example on finite probability spaces finding the deflators is essentially an exercise in linear algebra. Here, we would also like to mention that finite models often have the advantage that it is easier to find the crucial mathematical and economic structure (see also Malamud et al. [MTW07]).

Step 1. In a first step we construct the **state space securities** SS_1 and SS_2. A state space security for state s_i pays one unit if state s_i occurs at time 1. This state space securities are used to construct an arbitrage-free model. That is,

	SS_1	SS_2
market price Q	?	?
payout if in state s_1 at time 1	1	0
payout if in state s_2 at time 1	0	1

Since we have two states s_1 and s_2 we need two assets A and B to calibrate the model. Assume the following model for that assets:

	asset A	asset B
market price Q	1.65	1
payout if in state s_1 at time 1	3	2
payout if in state s_2 at time 1	1	0.5

The hedging/replicating portfolio for the state space securities can easily be found (solving linear equations, e.g. $SS_1 = xA + yB$ for appropriate choices x and y):

	units of asset A	units of asset B	market price Q
s_1 state security SS_1	-1	2	0.35
s_2 state security SS_2	4	-6	0.60

Note that this is similar to the derivation of the Arbitrage Pricing Theory model (see Ingersoll [Ing87], Chapter 7).

Hence, if we have another new risky asset $\mathbf{X}$ which pays 2 in state s_1 and 1 in state s_2, its price is given by

$$Q\left[\mathbf{X}\right] = 2 \cdot 0.35 + 1 \cdot 0.6 = 1.3. \qquad (2.28)$$

We consider now the zero coupon bond $\mathbf{Z}^{(1)}$. The zero coupon bond pays in both states 1:

$$Q\left[\mathbf{Z}^{(1)}\right] = 1 \cdot 0.35 + 1 \cdot 0.6 = 0.95, \qquad (2.29)$$

which leads to a risk-free return of $(0.95)^{-1} - 1 = 5.26\%$.

Step 2. Now we construct the deflators. Denote by $Q(s_i)$ the market price of the s_i state space security at time 0. Moreover, let $X_1(s_i)$ denote the payout at time 1 of the risky asset $\mathbf{X}$, if we are in state s_i at time 1. Hence the market price of $\mathbf{X}$ at time 0 is given by (see (2.28))

$$Q\left[\mathbf{X}\right] = \sum_{i=1}^{2} Q(s_i) \cdot X_1(s_i). \qquad (2.30)$$

So far we have not used any probabilities!
Now we assume that we are in state s_1 at time 1 with probability $p(s_1) \in (0, 1)$ and in state s_2 with probability $p(s_2) = 1 - p(s_1)$. Hence (2.30) can be rewritten as follows

$$Q\left[\mathbf{X}\right] = \sum_{i=1}^{2} Q(s_i) \cdot X_1(s_i) \qquad (2.31)$$

$$= \sum_{i=1}^{2} p(s_i) \cdot \frac{Q(s_i)}{p(s_i)} \cdot X_1(s_i)$$

$$= E\left[\frac{Q}{p} \cdot X_1\right].$$

Henceforth, define the random variable

$$\varphi_1 = \frac{Q}{p}, \qquad (2.32)$$

which immediately implies

$$Q\left[\mathbf{X}\right] = E\left[\varphi_1 \cdot X_1\right]. \qquad (2.33)$$

For an explicit choice of probabilities $p(s_i)$, the deflator φ_1 takes the following values:

	value of deflator φ_1	probability $p(s_i)$
state s_1 at time 1	0.7	0.5
state s_2 at time 1	1.2	0.5

Hence, alternatively to (2.29) we obtain for the value of the zero coupon bond

$$Q\left[\mathbf{Z}^{(1)}\right] = E\left[\varphi_1\right] = \sum_{i=1}^{2} \varphi_1(s_i) \cdot p(s_i) = 0.7 \cdot 0.5 + 1.2 \cdot 0.5 = 0.95. \quad (2.34)$$

2.3 Valuation at time $t > 0$

Postulate: Correct prices should eliminate the possibility to play games with cash flows (see also Remark 2.7).

We define the price process for a random vector $\mathbf{X} \in L_{n+1}^2(P)$ as follows $(t \in \{0, \ldots, n\})$:

$$Q_t\left[\mathbf{X}\right] = Q\left[\mathbf{X}|\mathcal{F}_t\right] = \frac{1}{\varphi_t} \cdot E\left[\sum_{k=0}^{n} \varphi_k \cdot X_k \,\middle|\, \mathcal{F}_t\right]. \quad (2.35)$$

Terminology.
The map $\mathbf{X} \mapsto Q_t[\mathbf{X}]$ gives a monetary value $Q_t[\mathbf{X}]$ at time t to the cash flow $\mathbf{X}$. Of course this monetary value is stochastic seen from time 0, it depends on $\mathcal{F}_t$. As we see below, this valuation process Q_t is done in a market-consistent way which leads to a risk neutral valuation scheme (see also Lemma 2.4 and Remark 2.7).

The justification of our price process Q_t uses an equilibrium principle or an arbitrage argument. Assume that we pay for cash flow $\mathbf{X}$ at time t the price $Q_t[\mathbf{X}]$. Hence, we generate a payment cash flow

$$Q_t\left[\mathbf{X}\right] \cdot \mathbf{Z}^{(t)} = (0, \ldots, 0, Q_t\left[\mathbf{X}\right], 0, \ldots, 0). \quad (2.36)$$

From today's point of view this payment stream has value

$$Q\left[Q_t\left[\mathbf{X}\right] \cdot \mathbf{Z}^{(t)}\right]. \quad (2.37)$$

Equilibrium requires, that

$$Q\left[\mathbf{X}\right] = Q\left[Q_t\left[\mathbf{X}\right] \cdot \mathbf{Z}^{(t)}\right], \quad (2.38)$$

since (based on today's information $\mathcal{F}_0$) the two payments streams should have the same value.

Suppose now that we play a game: We decide to pay (and buy) cash flow $\mathbf{X}$ only if an event $F_t \in \mathcal{F}_t$ occurs. Since from today's point of view we do not know, whether the event F_t occurs or not, we should have the following price equilibrium:

$$Q\left[\mathbf{X} \cdot 1_{F_t}\right] = Q\left[Q_t\left[\mathbf{X}\right] \cdot \mathbf{Z}^{(t)} \cdot 1_{F_t}\right].$$ (2.39)

Using deflators, we rewrite (2.39)

$$E\left[\sum_{k=0}^{n} \varphi_k X_k \cdot 1_{F_t}\right] = E\left[Q_t\left[\mathbf{X}\right] \varphi_t \cdot 1_{F_t}\right].$$ (2.40)

Since $(Q_t\left[\mathbf{X}\right]\varphi_t)$ is $\mathcal{F}_t$-measurable and equation (2.40) must hold true for all $F_t \in \mathcal{F}_t$, this is exactly the definition of conditional expectation given the σ-algebra $\mathcal{F}_t$. Henceforth, (2.40) implies (2.35), P-a.s.

We close this section with some remarks on "pure" financial risks. We have defined the traditional discount factors

$$D_{0,t} = Q\left[\mathbf{Z}^{(t)}\right] = E\left[\varphi_t\right].$$ (2.41)

For $m > k$, let $D_{k,m}$ stand for the discount from time m back to time k, *fixed* at time 0. The terminology forward refers to this fixing at an earlier time point. It is easy to see that we must have

$$D_{0,k} \cdot D_{k,m} = D_{0,m}.$$ (2.42)

The left-hand side of (2.42) is the price at time 0 for receiving $D_{k,m}$ at time k, and $D_{k,m}$ is the price for receiving 1 at time m (fixed at time 0 and to be paid at time k).

The right-hand side of (2.42) is the price at time 0 for receiving 1 at time m.

Hence we define forward discount factors for $m > k$:

$$D_{k,m} = \frac{D_{0,m}}{D_{0,k}}.$$ (2.43)

This is the forward price of a zero coupon bond with maturity m fixed at time 0 to be paid at time k ($\mathcal{F}_0$-measurable).

On the other hand, the value of a zero coupon bond with maturity m at time k (spot price) is given by ($\mathcal{F}_k$-measurable)

$$Q_k\left[\mathbf{Z}^{(m)}\right] = \frac{1}{\varphi_k} \cdot E\left[\varphi_m \,|\, \mathcal{F}_k\right] = E\left[\frac{\varphi_m}{\varphi_k}\,\middle|\, \mathcal{F}_k\right].$$ (2.44)

This is exactly (2.35) for a single deterministic payment in m.

Remark. In classical literature on financial mathematics in continuous time one often uses the notation $Q_k\left[\mathbf{Z}^{(m)}\right] = E\left[\varphi_m/\varphi_k\,|\,\mathcal{F}_k\right] = B(k,m) = E\left[\exp\left\{-\int_k^m r(u)du\right\}\,|\,\mathcal{F}_k\right]$, where r stands for the instantaneous stochastic interest rate.

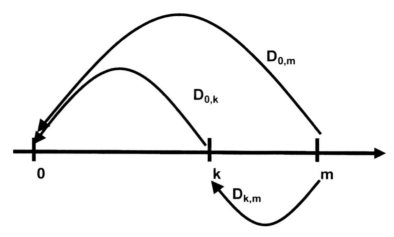

Fig. 2.4. Forward discount factors D_m and D_k

2.4 The meaning of basic reserves

Postulate: Correct basic reserves should eliminate the possibility to play games with an insurance contract.

Assume that an insurance contract is represented by the (stochastic) cash flow $\mathbf{X}$. We define for $k \leq n$

$$\mathbf{X}_{(k)} = (0, \ldots, 0, X_k, \ldots, X_n), \tag{2.45}$$

this is the remaining cash flow after time $k - 1$. $\mathbf{X}_{(k)}$ represents the amounts for which we have to build reserves at time $k - 1$, such that we are able to satisfy all contigent claims. Henceforth, the **reserves at time** $t \leq k - 1$ are defined as

$$R_k^{(t)} = R\left[\mathbf{X}_{(k)} \,\middle|\, \mathcal{F}_t\right] = Q_t[\mathbf{X}_{(k)}]. \tag{2.46}$$

On the one hand, $R_k^{(t)}$ corresponds to the conditionally expected monetary value of the the cash flow $\mathbf{X}_{(k)}$ viewed from time t. On the other hand, $R_k^{(t)}$ is used to predict the monetary value of the random variable $\mathbf{X}_{(k)}$. Therefore, $R_k^{(t)}$ is often called discounted "best estimate" reserves.

We determine $R_k^{(t)}$ similar as in the last section. We want to avoid that we can play games with the reserves. In particular, we consider the following game:

- Company A keeps the contract until the ultimate payment is done.
- Company B decides to sell the run-off of the liabilities at time $k - 1$ if an event $F_{k-1} \in \mathcal{F}_{k-1}$ occurs.

This implies that the two companies generate the following cash flows

0 ...	$k-1$	k	...	n

$$\mathbf{X}^{(A)} = \big(X_0, \ldots,\ \ X_{k-1},\ \ \ \ \ \ \ \ \ \ \ X_k,\ \ \ \ldots,\ \ \ X_n\big)$$
$$\mathbf{X}^{(B)} = \big(X_0, \ldots, X_{k-1} + R\left[\mathbf{X}_{(k)}\big|\mathcal{F}_{k-1}\right]\cdot 1_{F_{k-1}}, X_k\cdot 1_{F^c_{k-1}}, \ldots, X_n\cdot 1_{F^c_{k-1}}\big)$$

Hence, the price difference of these two strategies is given by

$$Q\left[\mathbf{X}^{(A)} - \mathbf{X}^{(B)}\right] = E\left[-\varphi_{k-1}R\left[\mathbf{X}_{(k)}\big|\mathcal{F}_{k-1}\right]\cdot 1_{F_{k-1}}\right] + E\left[\sum_{t=k}^{n}\varphi_t X_t \cdot 1_{F_{k-1}}\right]. \tag{2.47}$$

As in (2.39), we have that the two strategies based on the information $\mathcal{F}_0$ should have the same initial value. This implies that for all events $F_{k-1} \in \mathcal{F}_{k-1}$

$$E\left[\varphi_{k-1}\cdot R\left[\mathbf{X}_{(k)}\big|\mathcal{F}_{k-1}\right]\cdot 1_{F_{k-1}}\right] = E\left[\sum_{t=k}^{n}\varphi_t X_t \cdot 1_{F_{k-1}}\right]. \tag{2.48}$$

Hence, using the definition of conditional expectations, this justifies the following definition of the reserves:

$$R_k^{(k-1)} = R\left[\mathbf{X}_{(k)}\big|\mathcal{F}_{k-1}\right] = \frac{1}{\varphi_{k-1}}\cdot E\left[\sum_{t=k}^{n}\varphi_t \cdot X_t \bigg|\mathcal{F}_{k-1}\right] = Q_{k-1}\left[\mathbf{X}_{(k)}\right]. \tag{2.49}$$

Observe that we have the following self-financing property:

Corollary 2.6 (Self-financing property) *The following recursion holds*

$$E\left[\varphi_t \cdot \left(R_{t+1}^{(t)} + X_t\right)\bigg|\mathcal{F}_{t-1}\right] = \varphi_{t-1}\cdot R_t^{(t-1)}. \tag{2.50}$$

Remark.

- The classical actuarial theory with $\varphi_t = (1+i)^{-t}$ for some constant interest rate i (see (2.27)) forms a consistent theory but the deflators are not market-consistent, because they are far from observed economic behaviours.

Proof of Corollary 2.6. We have the following identity (using the $\mathcal{F}_t$-measurability of X_t and fundamental properties of conditional expectations)

$$E\left[\varphi_t \cdot \left(R_{t+1}^{(t)} + X_t\right)\bigg|\mathcal{F}_{t-1}\right] = E\left[\sum_{k=t}^{n}\varphi_k \cdot X_k \bigg|\mathcal{F}_{t-1}\right] = \varphi_{t-1}\cdot R_t^{(t-1)}. \tag{2.51}$$

This completes the proof of the corollary.

$\square$

2.5 Equivalent martingale measures

The price process defined in (2.35) gives in a natural way a martingale (that is, it satisfies the efficient market hypothesis in its strong form, see Remark 2.7):

Lemma 2.4. *The deflated price process*

$$(\varphi_t \cdot Q_t [\mathbf{X}])_{t=0,\dots,n} \quad forms \ an \ \mathcal{F}_t\text{-}martingale \ under \ P. \tag{2.52}$$

Proof. Since $\mathcal{F}_t \subset \mathcal{F}_{t+1}$ we have

$$E\left[\varphi_{t+1} \cdot Q_{t+1}[\mathbf{X}]\middle|\,\mathcal{F}_t\right] = E\left[E\left[\sum_{k=0}^{n} \varphi_k \cdot X_k \,\middle|\, \mathcal{F}_{t+1}\right]\middle|\,\mathcal{F}_t\right] \tag{2.53}$$

$$= E\left[\sum_{k=0}^{n} \varphi_k \cdot X_k \,\middle|\, \mathcal{F}_t\right] = \varphi_t \cdot Q_t[\mathbf{X}].$$

This finishes the proof of the lemma.

$\square$

Remarks on deflating and discounting.

- From the martingale property we immediately have

$$Q_t[\mathbf{X}] = \frac{1}{\varphi_t} E\left[\varphi_{t+1} \cdot Q_{t+1}[\mathbf{X}]\middle|\,\mathcal{F}_t\right] = E\left[\frac{\varphi_{t+1}}{\varphi_t} \cdot Q_{t+1}[\mathbf{X}]\,\middle|\,\mathcal{F}_t\right]. \tag{2.54}$$

This implies for the span-deflated price

$$Q_t[\mathbf{X}] = E\left[Y_{t+1} \cdot Q_{t+1}[\mathbf{X}]\middle|\,\mathcal{F}_t\right], \tag{2.55}$$

with span-deflator Y_{t+1} defined in (2.24). The (stochastic) span-deflator Y_{t+1} is $\mathcal{F}_{t+1}$-measurable, i.e. it is known only at the end of the time period $[t, t+1]$, and not at the beginning of the time period.
- We define the (stochastic) span discount known at the beginning of the time period $[t, t+1]$, i.e. which is observable on the market at time t:

$$D(\mathcal{F}_t) = E\left[Y_{t+1}|\mathcal{F}_t\right] = E\left[\frac{\varphi_{t+1}}{\varphi_t}\,\middle|\,\mathcal{F}_t\right]. \tag{2.56}$$

It is often convenient to rewrite (2.55) using the span discount $D(\mathcal{F}_t)$ instead of the span deflator Y_{t+1}. The reason is that the span discounts are eventually observable whereas span-deflators are always "hidden variables". The basic idea is to change the probability dP to dP^* such that we can change from span-deflators Y_{t+1} to observable span discounts $D(\mathcal{F}_t)$ at time t.

Lemma 2.5. *If we define the transformed measure P^* via the Radon-Nikodym derivative*

$$\frac{dP^*}{dP} = \prod_{t=0}^{n-1} \frac{Y_{t+1}}{D(\mathcal{F}_t)}, \tag{2.57}$$

then P^* is a probability measure.

Proof. We define

$$\xi_s = \prod_{t=0}^{s-1} \frac{Y_{t+1}}{D(\mathcal{F}_t)}. \tag{2.58}$$

Observe that $(\xi_s)_s$ is a martingale w.r.t. $(P, (\mathcal{F}_s)_s)$. But then we easily have

$$E^*[1] = E\left[\prod_{t=0}^{n-1} \frac{Y_{t+1}}{D(\mathcal{F}_t)}\right] = E\left[\xi_n\right] = E\left[\xi_1\right] = E\left[\frac{Y_1}{D(\mathcal{F}_0)}\right] = 1. \tag{2.59}$$

$\square$

Moreover, observe that

$$\left.\frac{dP^*}{dP}\right|_{\mathcal{F}_s} = \xi_s \qquad P\text{-a.s.} \tag{2.60}$$

Proof. Note that we have for any $\mathcal{F}_s$-measurable set A

$$P^*[A] = E\left[\xi_n \cdot 1_A\right] = E\left[E\left[\xi_n | \mathcal{F}_s\right] \cdot 1_A\right] = E\left[\xi_s \cdot 1_A\right]. \tag{2.61}$$

Therefore, ξ_s must coincide with density on $\mathcal{F}_s$.

$\square$

This then implies for $s < t$

$$E^*\left[Q_t\left[\mathbf{X}\right] | \mathcal{F}_s\right] = \frac{1}{\xi_s} \cdot E\left[\xi_t \cdot Q_t\left[\mathbf{X}\right] | \mathcal{F}_s\right] \qquad P\text{-a.s.} \tag{2.62}$$

Proof. Note that we have for any $\mathcal{F}_s$-measurable random variable $Z \geq 0$ (due to (2.61))

$$
\begin{aligned}
E^*\left[Z \cdot Q_t\left[\mathbf{X}\right]\right] &= E\left[Z \cdot \xi_n \cdot Q_t\left[\mathbf{X}\right]\right] \tag{2.63}\\
&= E\left[Z \cdot E\left[\xi_n \cdot Q_t\left[\mathbf{X}\right] | \mathcal{F}_s\right]\right]\\
&= E^*\left[Z \cdot \frac{1}{\xi_s} \cdot E\left[\xi_n \cdot Q_t\left[\mathbf{X}\right] | \mathcal{F}_s\right]\right]\\
&= E^*\left[Z \cdot \frac{1}{\xi_s} \cdot E\left[\xi_t \cdot Q_t\left[\mathbf{X}\right] | \mathcal{F}_s\right]\right],
\end{aligned}
$$

which is exactly the definition of conditional expectations w.r.t. P^*. This completes the proof.

$\square$

This immediately implies

$$E^* \left[Q_{t+1}\left[\mathbf{X} \right] \middle| \mathcal{F}_t \right] = \frac{1}{\xi_t} \cdot E \left[\xi_{t+1} \cdot Q_{t+1}\left[\mathbf{X} \right] \middle| \mathcal{F}_t \right] \qquad (2.64)$$

$$= \frac{1}{\xi_t} \cdot E \left[\xi_t \cdot \frac{Y_{t+1}}{D(\mathcal{F}_t)} \cdot Q_{t+1}\left[\mathbf{X} \right] \middle| \mathcal{F}_t \right]$$

$$= \frac{1}{D(\mathcal{F}_t)} \cdot E \left[Y_{t+1} \cdot Q_{t+1}\left[\mathbf{X} \right] \middle| \mathcal{F}_t \right]$$

$$= \frac{1}{D(\mathcal{F}_t)} \cdot Q_t\left[\mathbf{X} \right].$$

Hence we define the following discount vector

$$\varphi_t^* = \prod_{k=0}^{t-1} D\left(\mathcal{F}_k\right) = \frac{E\left[\varphi_1 \middle| \mathcal{F}_0 \right]}{\varphi_0} \ldots \frac{E\left[\varphi_t \middle| \mathcal{F}_{t-1} \right]}{\varphi_{t-1}} \qquad (2.65)$$

$$= \frac{E\left[\varphi_1 \middle| \mathcal{F}_0 \right]}{\varphi_1} \ldots \frac{E\left[\varphi_{t-1} \middle| \mathcal{F}_{t-2} \right]}{\varphi_{t-1}} \cdot E\left[\varphi_t \middle| \mathcal{F}_{t-1} \right],$$

and we find

$$E^* \left[\varphi_{t+1}^* \cdot Q_{t+1}\left[\mathbf{X} \right] \middle| \mathcal{F}_t \right] = \varphi_{t+1}^* \cdot E^* \left[Q_{t+1}\left[\mathbf{X} \right] \middle| \mathcal{F}_t \right] = \varphi_t^* \cdot Q_t\left[\mathbf{X} \right]. \qquad (2.66)$$

Note that the discount factor φ_{t+1}^* is now measurable w.r.t. $\mathcal{F}_t$. Hence, in contrast to (2.55) we have now an $\mathcal{F}_t$-measurable discount factor w.r.t. P^*. Moreover,

$$\left(\varphi_t^* \cdot Q_t\left[\mathbf{X} \right] \right)_{t=0,\ldots,n} \qquad (2.67)$$

is an $\mathcal{F}_t$-martingale w.r.t. P^* (equivalent martingale measure).

This implies for the one-period model

$$Q_0\left[\mathbf{X} \right] = D(\mathcal{F}_0) \cdot E^* \left[Q_1\left[\mathbf{X} \right] \right] = E\left[Y_1 \cdot Q_1\left[\mathbf{X} \right] \right]. \qquad (2.68)$$

Remark 2.7 (Fundamental Theorem of Asset Pricing)

- The **efficient market hypothesis** in its **strong form** assumes that the deflated price process

$$\widetilde{Q}_t = \varphi_t \cdot Q_t\left[\mathbf{X} \right] \qquad (2.69)$$

forms an $\mathcal{F}_t$-martingale under P. This means for the expected net gains $(t > s)$

$$E\left[\widetilde{Q}_t - \widetilde{Q}_s \middle| \mathcal{F}_s \right] = 0, \qquad (2.70)$$

which means that there exists no arbitrage strategy (which roots in the idea of risk-neutral valuation).

- The **efficient market hypothesis** in its **weak form** assumes that "there is no free lunch", i.e. there does not exist a self-financing trading strategy with positive expected gains and without any downside risk. In a finite discrete time model, this is equivalent to the existence of an equivalent martingale measure for the deflated price process (which rules out arbitrage) (see e.g. Theorem 2.6 in Lamberton–Lapeyre [LL91]), the proof is essentially an exercise in linear algebra. In a more general setting the characterization is more delicate (see Delbaen-Schachermayer [DS94] and Föllmer-Schied [FS04]).

- In complete markets, the equivalent martingale measure is unique, which implies that we have a perfect replication of the contingent claim and the calculation of the price is straight forward (see e.g. Theorem 3.4 in Lamberton–Lapeyre [LL91]).

- In incomplete markets, where we have more than one equivalent martingale measure, we need an economic model to decide on which measure to use (e.g. utility theory, super-hedge or efficient hedging (utility based models accepting some risks), see also Föllmer-Schied [FS04] or Malamud et al. [MTW07]).

Toy example (revisited).

In this subsection we revisit the toy example from Subsection 2.2.3. We transform our probability measure according to Lemma 2.5 (here we work in a one-period model):

$$p^*(s_i) = \frac{\varphi_1(s_i)}{E[\varphi_1]} \cdot p(s_i) = \frac{Q(s_i)}{Q[\mathbf{Z}^{(1)}]}. \tag{2.71}$$

Hence, from (2.30) and (2.33)

$$Q[\mathbf{X}] = E[\varphi_1 \cdot X_1] = \sum_{i=1}^{2} Q(s_i) \cdot X_1(s_i), \tag{2.72}$$

$$Q[\mathbf{X}] = E^*[\varphi_1^* \cdot X_1] = \sum_{i=1}^{2} Q(s_i) \cdot X_1(s_i), \tag{2.73}$$

with (see (2.65))

$$\varphi_1^* = \frac{Q}{p^*} = E[\varphi_1] = Q[\mathbf{Z}^{(1)}], \tag{2.74}$$

which is deterministic at time 0. Hence under P^* we have

$$Q[\mathbf{X}] = E^*[\varphi_1^* \cdot X_1] = Q[\mathbf{Z}^{(1)}] \cdot E^*[X_1]. \tag{2.75}$$

This leads to the following table $p^*(s_1) = 0.368$:

	$\mathbf{Z}^{(1)}$	asset A	asset B
market price Q	0.95	1.65	1.00
payout state s_1	1	3	2
payout state s_2	1	1	0.5
P^* expected payout	1	1.737	1.053
P^* expected return	5.26%	5.26%	5.26%

which is the martingale property of the discounted cash flow $Q\left[\mathbf{Z}^{(1)}\right] \cdot X_1$ w.r.t. P^*.

Conclusions:

- We have found three different ways to value cash flows $\mathbf{X}$:
  1. via a positive linear functional Q,
  2. via deflators φ under P,
  3. via risk neutral (martingale) measures.
- The advantage of using risk neutral measures is that the discount factor is a priori known, which means that we have state independent discount factors. The main disadvantage of using the risk neutral measure is that the concept is not straight forward, and that the risk neutral law changes under currency changes.
- By contrast, deflators are calculated using "real-world" probabilities. Moreover, as shown below, they clearly describe the dependence structures (also between deflator and cash flow). From a practical point of view, deflators allow for the modeling of options and guarantees in the policies, and are therefore prefered especially by actuaries that value life insurance products.

2.6 Technical and financial variables

For practical purposes in insurance applications it makes sense to factorize the payments X_k into an appropriate basis $\mathcal{U}_k$, $k = 0, 1, \ldots$. Assume that we can split the cash flow X_k as follows

$$X_k = \Lambda_k \cdot U_k, \quad k = 0, 1, \ldots. \tag{2.76}$$

The random variable U_k denotes the value of one unit of $\mathcal{U}_k$ and

$$\Lambda_k = \frac{X_k}{U_k}, \quad k = 0, 1, \ldots, \tag{2.77}$$

gives the number of units. This means that we measure insurance value/liabilities in units $\mathcal{U}_k$ which have price/value U_k. U_k is sometimes also called **numeraire** and the change from X_k to Λ_k can be interpreted as a change in the underlying basis.

Examples of units.

- Currencies like CHF, USD, EURO
- Indexed CHF (inflation index, salary index, claims inflation index, medical expenses index, etc.)
- stock index, real estates, etc.

Examples of technical events.

- death benefit, annuity payments, disability benefit.
- car accident compensation, fire claim
- medical expenses, workmen's compensation
- etc.

We would like to "factorize" such that we get independent random variables:

$$\mathcal{T} = (\mathcal{T}_t)_{t=0,\ldots,n} \quad \sigma\text{-filtration for the technical events,} \tag{2.78}$$
$$\mathcal{G} = (\mathcal{G}_t)_{t=0,\ldots,n} \quad \sigma\text{-filtration for the financial events,} \tag{2.79}$$

with for all t

$$\mathcal{F}_t = \mathcal{T}_t \otimes \mathcal{G}_t = \text{smallest } \sigma\text{-field containing all sets of } \mathcal{T}_t \text{ and } \mathcal{G}_t. \tag{2.80}$$

We assume that under P the two σ-filtrations $\mathcal{T}$ and $\mathcal{G}$ are independent, i.e. $\mathcal{F}_t$ can be split into a product of independent σ-fields, one covering technical risks and one covering financial risks. This decoupling is crucial in the sequel of this manuscript.

Assumption 2.8 *We assume that $\Lambda = (\Lambda_0, \ldots, \Lambda_n)$ only depends on $\mathcal{T}$ and $\mathbf{U} = (U_0, \ldots, U_n)$ only depends on $\mathcal{G}$. Moreover, we assume that we can factorize $\varphi_k = \varphi_k^{(\mathcal{T})} \cdot \varphi_k^{(\mathcal{G})}$ such that $\varphi^{(\mathcal{T})}$ only depends on $\mathcal{T}$ and $\varphi^{(\mathcal{G})}$ only depends on $\mathcal{G}$.*

Hence we split the problem into two independent problems (product measure)

$$dP = dP_\mathcal{T} \cdot dP_\mathcal{G}, \tag{2.81}$$

one for the technical risks and one for the financial risks.
Assumption 2.8 implies

$$\varphi_t \cdot Q_t[\mathbf{X}] = E\left[\sum_{k=0}^n \varphi_k \cdot X_k \,\middle|\, \mathcal{F}_t\right] \tag{2.82}$$
$$= E\left[\sum_{k=0}^n \varphi_k^{(\mathcal{T})} \cdot \Lambda_k \cdot \varphi_k^{(\mathcal{G})} \cdot U_k \,\middle|\, \mathcal{T}_t \otimes \mathcal{G}_t\right]$$
$$= \sum_{k=0}^n E\left[\varphi_k^{(\mathcal{T})} \Lambda_k \,\middle|\, \mathcal{T}_t\right] \cdot E\left[\varphi_k^{(\mathcal{G})} U_k \,\middle|\, \mathcal{G}_t\right].$$

Remarks.

- The expresssion $E\left[\varphi_k^{(\mathcal{T})} \Lambda_k \,\middle|\, \mathcal{T}_t\right]$ denotes the price of the insurance cover in units. $\varphi_k^{(\mathcal{T})}$ defines the loading (distortion) of the technical price. This price does not depend on the price of the units.

- The expression $E\left[\varphi_k^{(\mathcal{G})} U_k \Big| \mathcal{G}_t\right]$ denotes the price for one unit $\mathcal{U}_k$ at time t. $\varphi_k^{(\mathcal{G})}$ should be obtained from financial market data.
- We have separated the pricing problem into two independent pricing problems, one for pricing insurance cover in units and one for pricing units. This split looks very natural, but in practice one needs to be careful with its applications. Especially in non-life insurance, it is very difficult to find such an orthogonal split, since the severities of the claims often depend on the financial market and the split is non-trivial. For example, if we consider workmen's compensation (which pays the salary when someone is injured or sick), it is very difficult to describe the dependence structure between 1) salary height, 2) length of sickness (which may have mental cause), 3) state of the job market, 4) state of the financial market 5) political environment.
- The financial economy including insurance products could also be defined in other ways that would allow similar splits. For an example we refer to Malamud et al. [MTW07]. There one starts with a complete financial market described by the "financial" σ-algebra. Then one introduces insurance products that enlarge the underlying σ-algebra. This enlargement in general makes the market incomplete (but still arbitrage-free) and adds idiosyncratic risks to the economic model. Finally, one defines the "hedgeable" σ-algebra that exactly describes the part of the insurance claims that can be described via financial market movements. The remaining parts are then the insurance technical risks.

2.7 Conclusions on Chapter 2

We have developed **theoretical foundations of market consistent valuation** based on (possibly distorted) **expected values** (see (2.82)). The distorted probabilities will lead to the **price for risk**. The framework as developed is not the "full story" since it only gives the price for risk (the so-called (probably distorted) pure risk premium) for an insurance company.

It does not tell, how we have to organize the **risk bearing**.

The risk bearing, which guarantees the survival of an insurance company under certain adverse scenarios, can be organized as follows:

1. buying options and reinsurance, if available,
2. hedging options internally,
3. setting up risk bearing capital (solvency margin).

In practice, one has to be extremely careful in each application whether the price for risk resulting from the mathematical model is already sufficient to finance adverse scenarios.

Remark on the existing literature. There is a wide range of literature on the definition of market consistent values. Usually all these definitions are not very mathematical and slightly differ, e.g. market-consistent values should be realistic values, should serve for the exchange of two portfolios, etc. One has to be very careful with these definitions, e.g. do they include cost-of-capital charges, etc.

Our model gives a mathematical framework for a market-consistent valuation. Charges for the risk bearing can be integrated via distorted probabilities, however (as mentioned above) this does not solve the question of the organization of the risk bearing.

3

Valuation portfolio in life insurance

In this chapter we define the valuation portfolio for a life insurance portfolio. The construction is done with the help of an explicit example. We proceed in two steps: 1) Assume that the cash flow is deterministic, i.e. we have a deterministic life table, and only the value of the financial instruments describe a stochastic process. Hence we map the cash flow onto these financial instruments. 2) Assume that the cash flow is stochastic, i.e. that we have a stochastic life table. In that case we follow the construction in step 1, but we add loadings for the technical risks coming from the stochastic life table. This construction gives us a replicating portfolio (protected against technical risks) in terms of financial instruments.

3.1 Deterministic life insurance model

To define the valuation portfolio VaPo we start with a deterministic life insurance model where no technical risk is involved (see also [BBK04]). We assume that we have a deterministic mortality table (second order table) giving the mortalities without loadings. Let l_x denote the number of men alive aged x and d_x to number of men alive aged x which die before $x + 1$.

$$
\begin{array}{ccc}
l_x & & \\
\downarrow & \longrightarrow & d_x = l_x - l_{x+1} \\
l_{x+1} & & \\
\downarrow & \longrightarrow & d_{x+1} = l_{x+1} - l_{x+2} \\
l_{x+2} & & \\
\downarrow & \longrightarrow & d_{x+2} = l_{x+2} - l_{x+3} \\
\vdots & & \vdots
\end{array}
$$

Example 3.1 (Endowment insurance policy).

We assume that the initial sum insured is CHF 1, the age at the entry of the contract is $x = 50$ and the contract term is $n = 5$. Moreover we assume that:

- The annual premium $\Pi_t = \Pi$ $(t = 50, \ldots, 54)$ is due in non-indexed CHF at the beginning of each year.
- The benefits are indexed by a well-known index I_t $(t = 50, 51, \ldots 55)$ with $I_{50} = 1$.
  - Death benefit is the indexed maximum of I_t and $(1 + i)^{t-50}$ for some fixed minimal guarantee i.
  - Survival benefit is I_{55}, i.e. no minimal guarantee in case of survival.
  The benefits are paid at the end of the period.

This means, for example, that the survival benefit is given by a financial instrument **I** whose price is a stochastic process $(I_t)_t$. This index can be any financial instrument like a stock, a fund, etc. Hence, to hedge the survival benefit we need to by one unit of index **I** at the price $I_{50} = 1$ and it generates the (random) survival benefit I_{55} at time $t = 55$.

Hence the endowment contract gives the following cash flow diagram for $\mathbf{X} = (X_{50}, \ldots, X_{55})$: For initially l_{50} persons (for 1 person we divide by l_{50})

time	cash flow	premium	death benefit	survival benefit
50	X_{50}	$-l_{50} \cdot \Pi$		
51	X_{51}	$-l_{51} \cdot \Pi$	$d_{50} \cdot \left(I_{51} \vee (1+i)^1\right)$	
52	X_{52}	$-l_{52} \cdot \Pi$	$d_{51} \cdot \left(I_{52} \vee (1+i)^2\right)$	
53	X_{53}	$-l_{53} \cdot \Pi$	$d_{52} \cdot \left(I_{53} \vee (1+i)^3\right)$	
54	X_{54}	$-l_{54} \cdot \Pi$	$d_{53} \cdot \left(I_{54} \vee (1+i)^4\right)$	
55	X_{55}		$d_{54} \cdot \left(I_{55} \vee (1+i)^5\right)$	$l_{55} \cdot I_{55}$

Task: Value this endowment policy at the beginning and at successive years.

3.2 Valuation portfolio for deterministic life model

For Example 3.1 (deterministic life table) we construct a valuation portfolio. The construction of the valuation portfolio for this deterministic life tables is done in two steps. In a third step one can evaluate the cash value of the valuation portfolio.

Step 1. Define units, choose a basis.

- The premium Π is due at time t in non-indexed CHF. Hence, as units we choose the zero coupon bonds $Z^{(50)}, \ldots, Z^{(54)}$ (the units are denoted by $Z^{(t)}$, whereas the cash flow of the zero coupon bond $Z^{(t)}$ is denoted by $\mathbf{Z}^{(t)}$, see (2.26) and (3.4)).
- Survival benefit: Unit is the indexed fund **I** with price process $(I_t)_{t=50,\ldots,55}$.
- Death benefit $I_t \vee (1 + i)^{t-50}$ can be measured in an indexed fund **I** plus a put option on **I** with strike time t and strike $(1 + i)^{t-50}$. We denote this put option by $\mathrm{Put}^{(t)} = \mathrm{Put}^{(t)}(\mathbf{I}, (1 + i)^{t-50})$.

Hence we have the following units

$$(\mathcal{U}_1, \ldots, \mathcal{U}_{11}) \tag{3.1}$$
$$= \left(Z^{(50)}, \ldots, Z^{(54)}, \mathbf{I}, \mathrm{Put}^{(51)}\left(\mathbf{I}, (1+i)^1\right), \ldots, \mathrm{Put}^{(55)}\left(\mathbf{I}, (1+i)^5\right) \right),$$

i.e. we have that the total number of different units equals 11. These units play the role of the basis (financial instruments) in which we measure the insurance liabilities.

Step 2. Determine the number/amount of each unit.
At the beginning of the policy:

Valuation Scheme A (for l_{50} persons)

time	premium	death benefit	survival benefit
50	$-l_{50} \cdot \Pi \cdot Z^{(50)}$		
51	$-l_{51} \cdot \Pi \cdot Z^{(51)}$	$d_{50} \cdot \left(\mathbf{I} + \mathrm{Put}^{(51)}\left(\mathbf{I}, (1+i)^1\right)\right)$	
52	$-l_{52} \cdot \Pi \cdot Z^{(52)}$	$d_{51} \cdot \left(\mathbf{I} + \mathrm{Put}^{(52)}\left(\mathbf{I}, (1+i)^2\right)\right)$	
53	$-l_{53} \cdot \Pi \cdot Z^{(53)}$	$d_{52} \cdot \left(\mathbf{I} + \mathrm{Put}^{(53)}\left(\mathbf{I}, (1+i)^3\right)\right)$	
54	$-l_{54} \cdot \Pi \cdot Z^{(54)}$	$d_{53} \cdot \left(\mathbf{I} + \mathrm{Put}^{(54)}\left(\mathbf{I}, (1+i)^4\right)\right)$	
55		$d_{54} \cdot \left(\mathbf{I} + \mathrm{Put}^{(55)}\left(\mathbf{I}, (1+i)^5\right)\right)$	$l_{55} \cdot \mathbf{I}$

This immediately leads to the summary of units

Valuation Scheme B (for l_{50} persons)

unit $\mathcal{U}_i$	number of units
$Z^{(50)}$	$-l_{50} \cdot \Pi$
$Z^{(51)}$	$-l_{51} \cdot \Pi$
$Z^{(52)}$	$-l_{52} \cdot \Pi$
$Z^{(53)}$	$-l_{53} \cdot \Pi$
$Z^{(54)}$	$-l_{54} \cdot \Pi$
$\mathbf{I}$	$d_{50} + d_{51} + d_{52} + d_{53} + d_{54} + l_{55} = l_{50}$
$\mathrm{Put}^{(51)}\left(\mathbf{I}, (1+i)^1\right)$	d_{50}
$\mathrm{Put}^{(52)}\left(\mathbf{I}, (1+i)^2\right)$	d_{51}
$\mathrm{Put}^{(53)}\left(\mathbf{I}, (1+i)^3\right)$	d_{52}
$\mathrm{Put}^{(54)}\left(\mathbf{I}, (1+i)^4\right)$	d_{53}
$\mathrm{Put}^{(55)}\left(\mathbf{I}, (1+i)^5\right)$	d_{54}

Hence, our valuation portfolio VaPo($\mathbf{X}$) is an 11-dimensional vector (see Section 3.3) where we have specified a basis of financial instruments (dimension) and the number of instruments we need to hold to replicate the insurance claims.

Step 3. To obtain the (monetary) value of our cash flow we need to apply an accounting principle to the VaPo.

$\square$

Conclusion. In a first and second step, we decompose the liability cash flow $\mathbf{X} = (X_{50}, \ldots, X_{55})$ into a 11-dimensional vector VaPo($\mathbf{X}$), whose basis consists of financial instruments $\mathcal{U}_1, \ldots, \mathcal{U}_{11}$. Only in a third step, we calculate the monetary value of the cash flow $\mathbf{X}$ applying an accounting principle to VaPo($\mathbf{X}$), to the units $\mathcal{U}_i$, respectively.

Hence we have found the following general valuation procedure:

3.3 General valuation procedure for deterministic technical risks

1. For every policy with cash flow $\mathbf{X}$ (deterministic technical risk) we construct the VaPo($\mathbf{X}$) as follows: Define units $\mathcal{U}_i$ (basis of a multidimensional vector space) and determine the (deterministic) number $\lambda_i(\mathbf{X}) \in \mathbb{R}$ of each unit $\mathcal{U}_i$:

$$\mathbf{X} \mapsto \text{VaPo}(\mathbf{X}) = \sum_i \lambda_i(\mathbf{X}) \cdot \mathcal{U}_i. \qquad (3.2)$$

From a theoretical point of view the VaPo mapping is a multidimensional positive continuous linear functional that maps the insurance liabilities onto a replicating portfolio consisting of financial instruments.

2. Apply now an accounting principle $\mathcal{A}$ on the valuation portfolio to obtain a monetary value

$$\text{VaPo}(\mathbf{X}) \mapsto \mathcal{A}(\text{VaPo}(\mathbf{X})) = Q[\mathbf{X}] \in \mathbb{R}. \qquad (3.3)$$

This mapping must also be a positive continuous linear functional.

For the zero coupon bond we have ($\mathcal{U}_1 = Z^{(t)}$)

$$Q[\mathbf{Z}^{(t)}] = \mathcal{A}\left(\text{VaPo}(\mathbf{Z}^{(t)})\right) = \mathcal{A}\left(\lambda_1(\mathbf{Z}^{(t)}) \cdot Z^{(t)}\right) = \mathcal{A}\left(Z^{(t)}\right). \qquad (3.4)$$

The decomposition into these two steps adds enormously to the understanding and communication between actuaries and asset managers/investors. In a first step the actuary decomposes the insurance portfolio into financial instruments, in a second step the asset manager evaluates the financial instruments. Indeed, it is the key to a successful ALM-technique, and it clearly highlights the sources of uncertainties involved in the process. It also allocates the responsabilities for the uncertainties to the different parties involved.

For a cash flow $\mathbf{X}$ with no insurance technical risk involved we obtain

$$Q[\mathbf{X}] = \mathcal{A}(\text{VaPo}(\mathbf{X})) = \sum_i \lambda_i(\mathbf{X}) \cdot \mathcal{A}(\mathcal{U}_i), \qquad (3.5)$$

which is a positive continuous linear functional. One has to be a little bit careful with the positivity: In order to obtain a positive linear functional, we must have that $U_i = \mathcal{A}(\mathcal{U}_i) > 0$ as long as a policy is inforce, which must be kept in mind whenever the units are selected.

Remark. By linearity: Individual policies can be added up to a portfolio, i.e. individual cash flows $\mathbf{X}^{(m)}$ easily merge to

$$Q\left[\sum_m \mathbf{X}^{(m)}\right] = \sum_m \mathcal{A}\left(\mathrm{VaPo}(\mathbf{X}^{(m)})\right). \tag{3.6}$$

This means that we can value portfolios of a single contract as well as of the whole insurance company.

Examples of accounting principles $\mathcal{A}$. An accounting principle $\mathcal{A}$ attaches a value to the financial instruments. There are different ways to choose an appropriate accounting principle. In fact, choosing an appropriate accounting principle very much depends on the problem under considerations. We give two examples.

- Classical actuarial discounting. In many situation, for example in exchange with the regulator, the value of the financial instruments are determined by a mathematical model (such as amortized costs, etc.). If we choose the model where we discount with a fixed constant interest rate we denote the accounting principle by $\mathcal{D}$.
- In modern actuarial valuation, the financial instruments are often valued at an economic value, market value or value according to the IASB accounting rule. In general this means, that the value of the asset is essentially the price at which it can be exchanged on the financial market. If we use such an economic accounting principle we use the symbol $\mathcal{E}$.

3.4 Self-financing property of the VaPo (deterministic technical risk)

In (2.45) we have defined $\mathbf{X}_{(k)}$ as the remaining cash flow after time $k-1$. Moreover, define the cash flow

$$\mathbf{X}_k = X_k \cdot \mathbf{Z}^{(k)} = (0, \dots, 0, X_k, 0 \dots, 0). \tag{3.7}$$

Hence, note

$$\mathbf{X}_{(k)} = \mathbf{X}_{(k+1)} + \mathbf{X}_k. \tag{3.8}$$

and using the linearity of the valuation portfolio we have the following lemma.

Lemma 3.2 (Self-financing as portfolio).

$$\mathrm{VaPo}\left(\mathbf{X}_{(k)}\right) = \mathrm{VaPo}\left(\mathbf{X}_{(k+1)}\right) + \mathrm{VaPo}\left(\mathbf{X}_k\right). \tag{3.9}$$

Remark. At time k, the last term in (3.9) is simply cash value, i.e.

$$\mathrm{VaPo}\left(\mathbf{X}_k\right) = X_k \qquad \text{at time } k. \tag{3.10}$$

Studying now the values given by the accounting principle $\mathcal{A}$, we have by the linearity of $\mathcal{A}$ the following lemma:

Lemma 3.3.

$$\mathcal{A}\left(\mathrm{VaPo}\left(\mathbf{X}_{(k)}\right)\right) = \mathcal{A}\left(\mathrm{VaPo}\left(\mathbf{X}_{(k+1)}\right)\right) + \mathcal{A}\left(\mathrm{VaPo}\left(\mathbf{X}_k\right)\right). \tag{3.11}$$

For the evaluation of the valuation portfolio at time $m \leq k$ we define

$$\mathcal{A}_m\left(\mathrm{VaPo}(\mathbf{X}_{(k)})\right) = \mathcal{A}\left(\mathrm{VaPo}(\mathbf{X}_{(k)})\big|\,\mathcal{F}_m\right) = Q\left[\mathbf{X}_{(k)}\big|\,\mathcal{F}_m\right]. \tag{3.12}$$

If the valuation portfolio of $\mathbf{X}_k$ is evaluated at time k then

$$X_k = \frac{1}{\varphi_k} \cdot E\left[\varphi_k \cdot X_k |\, \mathcal{F}_k\right] = Q\left[\mathbf{X}_k |\, \mathcal{F}_k\right] = \mathcal{A}\left(\mathrm{VaPo}(\mathbf{X}_k)|\, \mathcal{F}_k\right), \tag{3.13}$$

hence

$$\mathcal{A}_k\left(\mathrm{VaPo}\left(\mathbf{X}_{(k)}\right)\right) = \mathcal{A}_k\left(\mathrm{VaPo}\left(\mathbf{X}_{(k+1)}\right)\right) + X_k, \tag{3.14}$$

which tells again, that the VaPo for $\mathbf{X}_k$ at time k is simply X_k. This observation is fundamental and should hold independently of the value assigned to the VaPo by the accounting principle $\mathcal{A}$.

For a more detailed analysis of the self-financing property in monetary value over time we refer to Subsection 6.2.

3.5 VaPo protected against technical risks

So far we have considered an ideal situation which is an important point of reference to measure deviations.

ideal	realistic	deviation
deterministic mortality	stochastic mortality	technical risk
VaPo	real investment portfolio $\mathcal{S}$	financial risk

In this section we want to consider technical risks. They come from the fact that the insurance liabilities are not deterministic. This means in our example that we have a stochastic mortality table.

For the deviations from the deterministic model (which are best estimates for the liabilities) we add a protection. Such a protection can be obtained e.g. via reinsurance products, risk loadings or risk bearing capital. The VaPo with this additional protection will be called **VaPo protected against technical risks**.

Let us return to our Example 3.1.

$$
\begin{array}{lll}
l_x & & \\
\downarrow & \longrightarrow & D_x = l_x - L_{x+1} \\
L_{x+1} & & \\
\downarrow & \longrightarrow & D_{x+1} = L_{x+1} - L_{x+2} \\
L_{x+2} & & \\
\downarrow & \longrightarrow & D_{x+2} = L_{x+2} - L_{x+3} \\
\vdots & & \vdots
\end{array}
$$

where now L_{x+k} and D_{x+k-1} are random variables for $k \geq 1$. From

$$D_{50} = l_{50} - L_{51}, \tag{3.15}$$

$$d_{50} = l_{50} - l_{51}, \tag{3.16}$$

we obtain

$$D_{50} - d_{50} = l_{51} - L_{51}, \tag{3.17}$$

which describes the deviations from the expected values. In fact, in a first step we use d_{50} as a predictor for the random variable D_{50}, and in a second step we need to study the prediction uncertainty or the deviations of the random variable around its predictor.

The valuation scheme A then reads as follows for the stochastic life table:

time	premium	death benefit	survival benefit
50	$-l_{50} \cdot \Pi \cdot Z^{(50)}$		
51	$-L_{51} \cdot \Pi \cdot Z^{(51)}$	$D_{50} \cdot \left(\mathbf{I} + \mathrm{Put}^{(51)} \left(\mathbf{I}, (1+i)^1 \right) \right)$	
52	$-L_{52} \cdot \Pi \cdot Z^{(52)}$	$D_{51} \cdot \left(\mathbf{I} + \mathrm{Put}^{(52)} \left(\mathbf{I}, (1+i)^2 \right) \right)$	
53	$-L_{53} \cdot \Pi \cdot Z^{(53)}$	$D_{52} \cdot \left(\mathbf{I} + \mathrm{Put}^{(53)} \left(\mathbf{I}, (1+i)^3 \right) \right)$	
54	$-L_{54} \cdot \Pi \cdot Z^{(54)}$	$D_{53} \cdot \left(\mathbf{I} + \mathrm{Put}^{(54)} \left(\mathbf{I}, (1+i)^4 \right) \right)$	
55		$D_{54} \cdot \left(\mathbf{I} + \mathrm{Put}^{(55)} \left(\mathbf{I}, (1+i)^5 \right) \right)$	$L_{55} \cdot \mathbf{I}$

Let us define the expected survival probabilities and the expected death probabilities (second order life table):

$$p_x = \frac{l_{x+1}}{l_x} \qquad \text{and} \qquad q_x = 1 - p_x = \frac{d_x}{l_x}. \tag{3.18}$$

Denote by $\text{VaPo}(\mathbf{X}_{(x+1)})$ the valuation portfolio for the cash flows after time x with deterministic technical risks (deterministic mortality table as defined in Section 3.2). I.e. $\text{VaPo}(\mathbf{X}_{(x+1)})$ denotes the valuation portfolio with the expected cash flows (L_x is replaced by its mean l_x).

If we allow for a stochastic survival in period $(50, 51]$ we have the following deviations from the expected VaPo (deterministic technical risks):

For $t = 51$ we obtain the following deviations form the expected payments

$$(D_{50} - d_{50}) \cdot \left(\mathbf{I} + \text{Put}^{(51)} \left(\mathbf{I}, (1+i)^1 \right) \right), \tag{3.19}$$

$$(l_{51} - L_{51}) \cdot \Pi \cdot Z^{(51)}, \tag{3.20}$$

$$(L_{51} - l_{51}) \cdot \frac{\text{VaPo}(\mathbf{X}_{(52)})}{l_{51}}, \tag{3.21}$$

if $\text{VaPo}(\mathbf{X}_{(52)})$ denotes the deterministic cash flows of our endowment policy after time $t = 51$ (according to Section 3.2). This means that we have deviations in the payments at time $t = 51$ due to the stochastic mortality, and then at $t = 51$, we start with a new basis of L_{51} men alive (instead of l_{51}), which gives a new expected VaPo after time $t = 51$ of

$$L_{51} \cdot \frac{\text{VaPo}(\mathbf{X}_{(52)})}{l_{51}}. \tag{3.22}$$

Using (3.17), equations (3.19)-(3.21) say that we need additional reserves of

$$(D_{50} - d_{50}) \cdot \left(\mathbf{I} + \text{Put}^{(51)} \left(\mathbf{I}, (1+i)^1 \right) + \Pi \cdot Z^{(51)} - \frac{\text{VaPo}(\mathbf{X}_{(52)})}{l_{51}} \right) \tag{3.23}$$

for a deviation from the expected life table within $(50, 51]$. Hence the portfolio at risk is

$$\mathbf{I} + \text{Put}^{(51)} \left(\mathbf{I}, (1+i)^1 \right) + \Pi \cdot Z^{(51)} - \frac{\text{VaPo}(\mathbf{X}_{(52)})}{l_{51}}. \tag{3.24}$$

We can now iterate this procedure: For $t = 52$ we have the following deviation from the expected VaPo. The expected VaPo starts now after $t = 51$ with the new basis of L_{51} men alive (we have to build the additional VaPo reserves for the new basis in (3.23)):

$$(D_{51} - q_{51} \cdot L_{51}) \cdot \left(\mathbf{I} + \text{Put}^{(52)} \left(\mathbf{I}, (1+i)^2 \right) \right), \tag{3.25}$$

$$(p_{51} \cdot L_{51} - L_{52}) \cdot \Pi \cdot Z^{(52)}, \tag{3.26}$$

$$(L_{52} - p_{51} \cdot L_{51}) \cdot \frac{\text{VaPo}(\mathbf{X}_{(53)})}{p_{51} \cdot L_{51}} \cdot \frac{L_{51}}{l_{51}}, \tag{3.27}$$

where the last term can be simplified to

$$\frac{\text{VaPo}(\mathbf{X}_{(53)})}{p_{51} \cdot L_{51}} \cdot \frac{L_{51}}{l_{51}} = \frac{\text{VaPo}(\mathbf{X}_{(53)})}{l_{52}}. \tag{3.28}$$

Hence we need for the deviation in $(51, 52]$ additional reserves of

$$(D_{51} - q_{51} \cdot L_{51}) \cdot \left(\mathbf{I} + \text{Put}^{(52)} \left(\mathbf{I}, (1+i)^2 \right) + \mathit{\Pi} \cdot Z^{(52)} - \frac{\text{VaPo}(\mathbf{X}_{(53)})}{l_{52}} \right). \tag{3.29}$$

And analogously for $t = 53, 54, 55$

$$(D_{52} - q_{52} \cdot L_{52}) \cdot \left(\mathbf{I} + \text{Put}^{(53)} \left(\mathbf{I}, (1+i)^3 \right) + \mathit{\Pi} \cdot Z^{(53)} - \frac{\text{VaPo}(\mathbf{X}_{(54)})}{l_{53}} \right),$$

$$(D_{53} - q_{53} \cdot L_{53}) \cdot \left(\mathbf{I} + \text{Put}^{(54)} \left(\mathbf{I}, (1+i)^4 \right) + \mathit{\Pi} \cdot Z^{(54)} - \frac{\text{VaPo}(\mathbf{X}_{(55)})}{l_{54}} \right),$$

$$(D_{54} - q_{54} \cdot L_{54}) \cdot \left(\mathbf{I} + \text{Put}^{(55)} \left(\mathbf{I}, (1+i)^5 \right) - \mathbf{I} \right). \tag{3.30}$$

Remark. One can see that when adding up in (3.23) and (3.29)-(3.30) the unit **I** cancels since $\text{VaPo}(\mathbf{X}_{(x+1)})$ contains exactly l_x units of **I**. This is immediately clear, because the number of **I**, we need to buy at the beginning of the policy, does not depend on the mortality table (see Valuation Scheme B on page 31).

Hence we find the following portfolios at risk:

$$t = 51 : \mathbf{I} + \text{Put}^{(51)} \left(\mathbf{I}, (1+i)^1 \right) + \mathit{\Pi} \cdot Z^{(51)} - \frac{\text{VaPo}(\mathbf{X}_{(52)})}{l_{51}}, \tag{3.31}$$

$$t = 52 : \mathbf{I} + \text{Put}^{(52)} \left(\mathbf{I}, (1+i)^2 \right) + \mathit{\Pi} \cdot Z^{(52)} - \frac{\text{VaPo}(\mathbf{X}_{(53)})}{l_{52}}, \tag{3.32}$$

$$t = 53 : \mathbf{I} + \text{Put}^{(53)} \left(\mathbf{I}, (1+i)^3 \right) + \mathit{\Pi} \cdot Z^{(53)} - \frac{\text{VaPo}(\mathbf{X}_{(54)})}{l_{53}}, \tag{3.33}$$

$$t = 54 : \mathbf{I} + \text{Put}^{(54)} \left(\mathbf{I}, (1+i)^4 \right) + \mathit{\Pi} \cdot Z^{(54)} - \frac{\text{VaPo}(\mathbf{X}_{(55)})}{l_{54}}, \tag{3.34}$$

$$t = 55 : \mathbf{I} + \text{Put}^{(55)} \left(\mathbf{I}, (1+i)^5 \right) - \mathbf{I}. \tag{3.35}$$

This means, if we take for example the period $(52, 53]$: If more people die than expected $(D_{52} > q_{52} \cdot L_{52})$ we have to pay an additional death benefit of

$$(D_{52} - q_{52} \cdot L_{52}) \cdot \left(\mathbf{I} + \text{Put}^{(53)} \left(\mathbf{I}, (1+i)^3 \right) \right). \tag{3.36}$$

On the other hand for all these people the contracts are terminated which means that our liablities are reduced by

$$(D_{52} - q_{52} \cdot L_{52}) \cdot \left(-\mathit{\Pi} \cdot Z^{(53)} + \frac{\text{VaPo}(\mathbf{X}_{(54)})}{l_{53}} \right). \tag{3.37}$$

These technical risks are now protected against adverse developments by adding a security loading. This gives us the following **reinsurance premium loadings as a portfolio**:

$$\text{RPP}_{50} = l_{50} \cdot (q_{50}^* - q_{50})$$
$$\cdot \left(\mathbf{I} + \text{Put}^{(51)} \left(\mathbf{I}, (1+i)^1 \right) + \Pi \cdot Z^{(51)} - \frac{\text{VaPo}(\mathbf{X}_{(52)})}{l_{51}} \right),$$

$$\text{RPP}_{51} = l_{51} \cdot (q_{51}^* - q_{51})$$
$$\cdot \left(\mathbf{I} + \text{Put}^{(52)} \left(\mathbf{I}, (1+i)^2 \right) + \Pi \cdot Z^{(52)} - \frac{\text{VaPo}(\mathbf{X}_{(53)})}{l_{52}} \right),$$

$$\text{RPP}_{52} = l_{52} \cdot (q_{52}^* - q_{52})$$
$$\cdot \left(\mathbf{I} + \text{Put}^{(53)} \left(\mathbf{I}, (1+i)^3 \right) + \Pi \cdot Z^{(53)} - \frac{\text{VaPo}(\mathbf{X}_{(54)})}{l_{53}} \right),$$

$$\text{RPP}_{53} = l_{53} \cdot (q_{53}^* - q_{53})$$
$$\cdot \left(\mathbf{I} + \text{Put}^{(54)} \left(\mathbf{I}, (1+i)^4 \right) + \Pi \cdot Z^{(54)} - \frac{\text{VaPo}(\mathbf{X}_{(55)})}{l_{54}} \right),$$

$$\text{RPP}_{54} = l_{54} \cdot (q_{54}^* - q_{54}) \cdot \left(\mathbf{I} + \text{Put}^{(55)} \left(\mathbf{I}, (1+i)^5 \right) - \mathbf{I} \right), \qquad (3.38)$$

where $q_x^* - q_x$ denote the loadings charged by the reinsurer against technical risks, and l_x is the number of units, we need to buy. q_x^* can be interpreted as the yearly renewable term (YRT) rates charged by the reinsurer.

Valuation Portfolio protected against technical risks is now defined as

$$\text{VaPo}^{prot}(\mathbf{X}) = \text{VaPo}(\mathbf{X}) + \sum_{t=50}^{54} \text{RPP}_t. \qquad (3.39)$$

Remarks.

- For a monetary reinsurance premium we need to apply an accounting principle $\mathcal{A}$ to the reinsurance premium portfolio (yearly renewable term):

$$\Pi_t^R = \mathcal{A}(\text{RPP}_t) \qquad (3.40)$$
$$= l_t \cdot (q_t^* - q_t)$$
$$\cdot \mathcal{A} \left(\mathbf{I} + \text{Put}^{(t+1)} \left(\mathbf{I}, (1+i)^{t-50+1} \right) + \Pi \cdot Z^{(t+1)} - \frac{\text{VaPo}(\mathbf{X}_{(t+2)})}{l_{t+1}} \right).$$

- There are now different possibilities to determine the premium: We could choose an actuarial accounting principle $\mathcal{D}$ or an economic accounting principle $\mathcal{E}$ (which gives an economic yearly renewable term, see also page 33). This idea opens interesting *new reinsurance products*: Offer a reinsurance cover against technical risks in terms of a valuation portfolio.
- A static hedging strategy is to invest the reinsurance premium into the reinsurance valuation portfolios.

3.6 Back to the basic model

In Chapter 2 we have chosen a deflator

$$\varphi = (\varphi_0, \ldots, \varphi_n) \tag{3.41}$$

to value a cash flow $\mathbf{X} = (X_0, \ldots, X_n)$. The basic hypothesis was that φ and $\mathbf{X}$ are $(\mathcal{F}_t)_{t=0,\ldots,n}$ adapted. Moreover, we have assumed that in our probability space we can decompose $\mathcal{F}_t$ into two independent σ-algebras $\mathcal{T}_t$ and $\mathcal{G}_t$ such that (componentwise multiplication)

$$\mathbf{X} = \mathbf{\Lambda} \cdot \mathbf{U}, \tag{3.42}$$
$$\varphi = \varphi^{(\mathcal{T})} \cdot \varphi^{(\mathcal{G})}, \tag{3.43}$$

and such that $\sigma(\mathbf{\Lambda}), \sigma(\varphi^{(\mathcal{T})}) \subset \mathcal{T}$ and $\sigma(\mathbf{U}), \sigma(\varphi^{(\mathcal{G})}) \subset \mathcal{G}$. To avoid ambiguity we assume that the expectation of the technical distortion is 1,

$$E\left[\varphi_t^{(\mathcal{T})}\right] = 1 \tag{3.44}$$

for all t. Below, we will see that for the protected valuation portfolio this technical distortion becomes important.

The VaPo construction in this chapter has now led to a multidimensional approach, i.e. the cash flow $\mathbf{X}$ is decomposed into a vector consisting of different financial instruments/units (see (3.2))

$$\mathbf{X} \mapsto \sum_{i=1}^{p} \Lambda_i(\mathbf{X}) \cdot \mathcal{U}_i, \tag{3.45}$$

if $\mathcal{U}_1, \ldots, \mathcal{U}_p$ represent the p financial instruments by which $\mathbf{X}$ can be described, and Λ_i the (random) number of units $\mathcal{U}_i$. The value/price of $\mathcal{U}_i$ is denoted by U_i and is independent of $\mathcal{T}$. If we now use vector notation, (3.45) can be rewritten as (we have linear mappings)

$$\mathbf{X} = \begin{pmatrix} X_0 \\ X_1 \\ \vdots \\ X_n \end{pmatrix} \mapsto \sum_{i=1}^{p} \begin{pmatrix} \Lambda_i(\mathbf{X}_0) \\ \Lambda_i(\mathbf{X}_1) \\ \vdots \\ \Lambda_i(\mathbf{X}_n) \end{pmatrix}^{T} \cdot \begin{pmatrix} \mathcal{U}_i \\ \mathcal{U}_i \\ \vdots \\ \mathcal{U}_i \end{pmatrix}, \tag{3.46}$$

where $\mathbf{X}_t = X_t \cdot \mathbf{Z}^{(t)} = (0, \ldots, 0, X_t, 0, \ldots, 0)$.

For the **VaPo construction seen from time 0** we have then replaced the random $\Lambda_i(\mathbf{X}_k)$ by deterministic numbers:

$$\Lambda_i(\mathbf{X}_k) \mapsto l_{i,k} = l_{i,k}^{(0)} = E\left[\Lambda_i(\mathbf{X}_k) \mid \mathcal{T}_0\right], \tag{3.47}$$

if $\Lambda_i(\mathbf{X}_k)$ is deterministic as in Section 3.1 then we have $\Lambda_i(\mathbf{X}_k) = \lambda_i(\mathbf{X}_k) = l_{i,k}$ (see (3.2)).

For the **VaPo protected against technical risks** (seen from time zero) we replace $\Lambda_i(\mathbf{X}_k)$ by the following deterministic numbers:

$$\Lambda_i(\mathbf{X}_k) \;\longmapsto\; l_{i,k}^* = l_{i,k}^{*,0} = E\left[\varphi_k^{(T)} \cdot \Lambda_i(\mathbf{X}_k)\,\middle|\,\mathcal{T}_0\right], \tag{3.48}$$

which adds a loading on $l_{i,k}$ for technical risks. If $\Lambda_i(\mathbf{X}_k)$ is deterministic as in Section 3.1 then we have $\Lambda_i(\mathbf{X}_k) = \lambda_i(\mathbf{X}_k) = l_{i,k} = l_{i,k}^*$ due to (3.44), i.e. we do not need a loading for technical risks. The loading in $l_{i,k}^*$ could also have been chosen directly, not via the definition of a deflator. This gives now

$$\text{VaPo}\,(\mathbf{X}) = \sum_{i=1}^{p} \begin{pmatrix} l_{i,0} \\ \vdots \\ l_{i,n} \end{pmatrix}^T \cdot \begin{pmatrix} \mathcal{U}_i \\ \vdots \\ \mathcal{U}_i \end{pmatrix} \tag{3.49}$$

and

$$\text{VaPo}^{prot}\,(\mathbf{X}) = \sum_{i=1}^{p} \begin{pmatrix} l_{i,0}^* \\ \vdots \\ l_{i,n}^* \end{pmatrix}^T \cdot \begin{pmatrix} \mathcal{U}_i \\ \vdots \\ \mathcal{U}_i \end{pmatrix}. \tag{3.50}$$

Applying an accounting principle $\mathcal{A}$ onto the VaPo, to the financial intruments $\mathcal{U}_i$ respectively, gives then a monetary value for the reserves.

Remark. It is important to see that the valuation portfolio construction in (3.47) is seen from time 0. If the cash flows have no technical risks (as in Section 3.3) there are no deviations in $\Lambda_i(\mathbf{X})$ over time, which means that $l_{i,k}$ is constant in time. But if we have technical risks involved, then

$$l_{i,k}^{(m)} = E\left[\Lambda_i(\mathbf{X}_k)\,\middle|\,\mathcal{T}_m\right], \tag{3.51}$$

$$l_{i,k}^{*,m} = E\left[\varphi_k^{(T)} \cdot \Lambda_i(\mathbf{X}_k)\,\middle|\,\mathcal{T}_m\right] \tag{3.52}$$

are functions of time (see also Chapter 6). This then leads to time dependent valuation portfolios

$$\text{VaPo}_{(m)}\,(\mathbf{X}) \quad \text{and} \quad \text{VaPo}^{prot}_{(m)}\,(\mathbf{X}). \tag{3.53}$$

3.7 Conclusion on Chapter 3

We have decomposed the cash flow $\mathbf{X}$ in two steps:

1. Choose a multidimensional vector space whose basis consists of financial instruments $\mathcal{U}_1, \ldots, \mathcal{U}_p$.

2. Express the cash flow **X** as a vector in this vector space. The number of each unit is determined by the expected number of units (where the expectation is calculated with possibly distorted probabilities).

Calculating the monetary value of the valuation portfolio is then the third step where we use an accounting principle to give values to the vectors in the multidimensional vector space.

We should mention that we have constructed our VaPo for a very easy example. In practice the VaPo construction is much more difficult because, for example, 1) Modelling options and guarantees can become very difficult. 2) Often one has not the necessary information on single policies in the portfolio (e.g. collective policies). Moreover, in practice one faces a lot of problems about data storing and data management since the volume of the data can become very large.

Finally, we mention that we can also construct the VaPo if the financial instruments do not exist on the financial market, e.g. a 41-years zero coupon bond. The VaPo construction still works. However, calculating the monetary value of the VaPo is not straightforward, if the instruments do not exist on the financial market.

3.8 Examples

In this section we give a numerical example to the deterministic Example 3.1 (endowment insurance policy). Note that the mathematical details for the evaluation of the accounting principles are given in Chapter 4, below.

For the deterministic life table we choose Table 3.1.

time	survival	death
50	$l_{50} = 1'000$	
51	$l_{51} = 996$	$d_{50} = 4$
52	$l_{52} = 991$	$d_{51} = 5$
53	$l_{53} = 986$	$d_{52} = 5$
54	$l_{54} = 981$	$d_{53} = 5$
55	$l_{55} = 975$	$d_{54} = 6$

Table 3.1. Deterministic life table, portfolio of 1'000 insured

Example 3.4 (Equity-linked life insurance).

We choose an equity-linked life insurance product. Assume that I_s denotes the price process of the equity index **I** (see (4.9)) in the economic world $\mathcal{E}$. That is, we choose an accounting principle $\mathcal{E}$ that corresponds to market prices, moreover $\mathcal{E}_s$ denotes these market prices at time s, henceforth

$$I_s = \mathcal{E}_s\left(\mathbf{I}\right) = \mathcal{E}\left(\mathbf{I}\middle|\mathcal{G}_s\right), \tag{3.54}$$

and that $Z_s^{(t)}$ $(s \le t)$ denotes the price process of the zero coupon bond paying 1 at time t. I.e.

$$Z_s^{(t)} = Q_s\left[\mathbf{Z}^{(t)}\right] = Q\left[\mathbf{Z}^{(t)}\middle|\mathcal{G}_s\right] = \mathcal{E}_s\left(Z^{(t)}\right) = \mathcal{E}\left(Z^{(t)}\middle|\mathcal{G}_s\right), \tag{3.55}$$

where $\mathbf{Z}^{(t)}$ is the cash flow of the zero coupon bond $Z^{(t)}$ (see (4.10)). Assume that the zero coupon bond yield curves $R(s,t)$ at time s are given by

$$Z_s^{(t)} = \exp\left\{-(t-s)\cdot R(s,t)\right\} \iff R(s,t) = \frac{-1}{t-s}\cdot\log Z_s^{(t)}. \tag{3.56}$$

Considering historical data we observe (source of zero coupon bond yield curves given by the Schweizerische Nationalbank [SNB]): see Table 3.2.

s	$\ln(I_s/I_{s-1})$	$R(s,t)$				
		$t-s=1$	$t-s=2$	$t-s=3$	$t-s=4$	$t-s=5$
1996	12.99%	1.94%	2.42%	2.79%	3.12%	3.42%
1997	13.35%	1.82%	1.92%	2.20%	2.48%	2.74%
1998	22.11%	1.71%	1.81%	1.95%	2.10%	2.27%
1999	5.41%	2.21%	2.06%	2.21%	2.31%	2.42%
2000	2.02%	3.37%	3.52%	3.53%	3.56%	3.60%
2001	8.60%	2.00%	2.85%	2.90%	2.96%	3.02%
2002	−12.41%	0.69%	1.84%	2.14%	2.38%	2.57%
2003	−14.83%	0.58%	0.79%	1.14%	1.46%	1.72%
2004	15.87%	0.99%	1.11%	1.42%	1.70%	1.94%
2005	1.83%	1.41%	1.14%	1.32%	1.48%	1.62%
average	5.49%	1.67%	1.95%	2.16%	2.35%	2.53%

Table 3.2. Equity index and yield curve of the zero coupon bond

We assume that our endowment insurance policy starts in year 2000, i.e. we identify the starting point at age $x = 50$ with the year $t_0 = 2000$.

Assume that the guaranteed interest rate is $i = 2\%$.

To adopt the option pricing formula to the case of non-constant interest rates we transform our price process I_s by a change of the numéraire (see also Subsection 4.3.2) and consider for $t_0 \le s \le t$

$$\widetilde{I}_s = \frac{I_s}{Z_s^{(t)}} \qquad \text{for fixed } t. \tag{3.57}$$

Now we need to choose a stochastic model for the price process $\widetilde{I}_s$: In order to apply classical financial mathematics we switch to a continuous time model. We assume that, under the risk neutral measure, $\widetilde{I}_s$ is a martingale satisfying the following stochastic differential equation

$$d\widetilde{I}_s = \sigma \cdot \widetilde{I}_s \cdot dB_s, \tag{3.58}$$

where B_s is a standard Brownian motion under the risk neutral measure. Hence using Ito calculus, $\widetilde{I}_s$ can be rewritten as follows (see e.g. Subsection 3.4.3 in [LL91])

$$\widetilde{I}_s = \widetilde{I_{t_0}} \cdot \exp\left\{-\frac{\sigma^2}{2} \cdot (s - t_0) + \sigma \cdot B_{s-t_0}\right\}. \tag{3.59}$$

Using the general option pricing formula for European put options (see e.g. Section 9.4 in [EK99]) we obtain the price process

$$\mathcal{E}_s\left(\mathrm{Put}^{(t)}\left(\mathbf{I}, (1+i)^{t-t_0}\right)\right) = K_s^{(t)} \cdot \Phi\left(-d_2(s,t)\right) - I_s \cdot \Phi\left(-d_1(s,t)\right), \tag{3.60}$$

with Φ standard Gaussian distribution and

$$K_s^{(t)} = (1+i)^{t-t_0} \cdot Z_s^{(t)}, \tag{3.61}$$

$$d_1(s,t) = \frac{\log\left(I_s/K_s^{(t)}\right) + \sigma^2(t-s)/2}{\sigma\sqrt{t-s}}, \tag{3.62}$$

$$d_2(s,t) = d_1(s,t) - \sigma\sqrt{t-s}. \tag{3.63}$$

Remark. For $Z_s^{(t)} = \exp\{-r \cdot (t-s)\}$ with $r > 0$ constant (3.60) is the well-known Black-Scholes forumla.

We choose I_s and $Z_s^{(t)}$ according to Table 3.2 with $I_{t_0} = 1$ and $\sigma = 15\%$ and obtain the following prices for the put options (observe that in year $t_0 = 2000$ we have a rather high yield $R(t_0, t)$, which gives a low price for our put option): see Table 3.3.

	$t-s=1$	$t-s=2$	$t-s=3$	$t-s=4$	$t-s=5$
$s = 2000$	0.053	0.069	0.080	0.088	0.093
$s = 2001$	0.034	0.051	0.066	0.076	
$s = 2002$	0.117	0.131	0.144		
$s = 2003$	0.249	0.267			
$s = 2004$	0.140				

Table 3.3. Prices $\mathcal{E}_s\left(\mathrm{Put}^{(t)}\left(\mathbf{I}, (1+i)^{t-t_0}\right)\right)$

Now we calculate the monetary value of the valuation portfolio of $\mathbf{X}$: Assume that the survival and death benefit capital (before index-linking) is 100'000. Hence we require (premium equivalence principle)

$$\mathcal{E}_{t_0}\left(\mathrm{VaPo}\left(\mathbf{X}\right)\right) = Q_{t_0}\left[\mathbf{X}\right] \stackrel{(!)}{=} 0, \tag{3.64}$$

which gives the market-consistent pure risk premium $\Pi = 21'667$.

Now we consider the valuation portfolios at different times $t_0 \leq s \leq t - 1$. Denote by $\mathbf{X}_{(s+1)} = (0, \ldots, X_{s+1}, \ldots, X_t)$ the cash flow after time s.

$$\mathcal{E}_s^{(+)} = \mathcal{E}_s \left(\text{VaPo} \left(\mathbf{X}_{(s+1)} \right) - \Pi \cdot Z^{(s)} \right) \tag{3.65}$$
$$= \mathcal{E}_s \left(\text{VaPo} \left(\mathbf{X}_{(s+1)} \right) \right) - \Pi = Q_s \left[\mathbf{X}_{(s+1)} \right] - \Pi,$$

is the monetary value before the premium Π has been paid at time s, and

$$\mathcal{E}_s^{(-)} = \mathcal{E}_s \left(\text{VaPo} \left(\mathbf{X}_{(s+1)} \right) \right) = Q_s \left[\mathbf{X}_{(s+1)} \right], \tag{3.66}$$

is the monetary value after the premium Π has been paid at time s. Of course $\mathcal{E}_{t_0}^{(+)} = \mathcal{E}_{t_0} \left(\text{VaPo} \left(\mathbf{X} \right) \right) = 0$. This gives the following results for the monetary values of the valuation portfolios: see Table 3.4.

	$\mathcal{E}_s^{(+)}$	$\mathcal{E}_s^{(-)}$
$s = 2000$	0	21'666'637
$s = 2001$	26'370'714	47'950'684
$s = 2002$	32'423'186	53'894'823
$s = 2003$	39'619'061	60'982'365
$s = 2004$	74'244'766	95'499'737

Table 3.4. Development of the monetary values of the valuation portfolios

For the valuation portfolio protected against technical risks, we proceed as follows: we define p_x and q_x as in (3.18). Moreover we choose $p_x^* = 1.5 \cdot p_x$. Hence we consider the premium for the yearly renewable term Π_s^R defined in (3.40) for our accounting principle $\mathcal{E}_{t_0}$. This gives the following monetary reinsurance loadings at time t_0: see Table 3.5.

	Π_s^R
$s = 2000$	167'885
$s = 2001$	162'340
$s = 2002$	115'180
$s = 2003$	68'723
$s = 2004$	27'818

Table 3.5. monetary yearly renewable terms premium

Example 3.5 (Wage index).

In non-life insurance the products are rather linked to other indices like the inflation index, wage index, the consumer price index or a medical expenses index. As index we choose the wage index (source [SNB]): see Table 3.6.

s	$\frac{I_s}{I_{s-1}} - 1$	$R(s,t)$				
		$t-s=1$	$t-s=2$	$t-s=3$	$t-s=4$	$t-s=5$
1996	1.30%	1.94%	2.42%	2.79%	3.12%	3.42%
1997	1.26%	1.82%	1.92%	2.20%	2.48%	2.74%
1998	0.47%	1.71%	1.81%	1.95%	2.10%	2.27%
1999	0.69%	2.21%	2.06%	2.21%	2.31%	2.42%
2000	0.29%	3.37%	3.52%	3.53%	3.56%	3.60%
2001	1.26%	2.00%	2.85%	2.90%	2.96%	3.02%
2002	2.48%	0.69%	1.84%	2.14%	2.38%	2.57%
2003	1.79%	0.58%	0.79%	1.14%	1.46%	1.72%
2004	1.40%	0.99%	1.11%	1.42%	1.70%	1.94%
2005	0.93%	1.41%	1.14%	1.32%	1.48%	1.62%
average	1.19%	1.67%	1.95%	2.16%	2.35%	2.53%

Table 3.6. Wage inflation index and yield curve of the zero coupon bond

This time we choose as minimal guaranteed interest rate of $i = 1.5\%$. For the volatility we choose $\sigma = 1\%$.
This implies that the market-consistent pure risk premium $\Pi = 21'624$ and that the put prices are given by: see Table 3.7.

	$t-s=1$	$t-s=2$	$t-s=3$	$t-s=4$	$t-s=5$
$s = 2000$	$1.16 \cdot 10^{-4}$	$8.26 \cdot 10^{-6}$	$8.42 \cdot 10^{-7}$	$7.36 \cdot 10^{-8}$	$4.74 \cdot 10^{-9}$
$s = 2001$	$2.82 \cdot 10^{-3}$	$2.28 \cdot 10^{-4}$	$6.14 \cdot 10^{-5}$	$1.39 \cdot 10^{-5}$	
$s = 2002$	$4.60 \cdot 10^{-3}$	$1.21 \cdot 10^{-3}$	$4.75 \cdot 10^{-4}$		
$s = 2003$	$3.72 \cdot 10^{-3}$	$8.27 \cdot 10^{-3}$			
$s = 2004$	$2.43 \cdot 10^{-3}$				

Table 3.7. Prices $\mathcal{E}_s \left(\text{Put}^{(t)} \left(\mathbf{I}, (1+i)^{t-t_0} \right) \right)$

Observe that the premium Π and the put prices are smaller in the wage index example than in the equity-linked example. This comes from the fact that the choice of σ is much smaller in the second example.
The monetary values of the valuation portfolios are then given by: see Table 3.8.

	$\mathcal{E}_s^{(+)}$	$\mathcal{E}_s^{(-)}$
$s = 2000$	0	21'624'505
$s = 2001$	18'723'288	40'261'295
$s = 2002$	39'780'582	61'210'467
$s = 2003$	61'740'997	83'062'759
$s = 2004$	83'857'251	105'070'890

Table 3.8. Development of the monetary values of the valuation portfolios

And the reinsurance loadings are given by: see Table 3.9.

	Π_s^R
$s = 2000$	157'404
$s = 2001$	145'186
$s = 2002$	95'278
$s = 2003$	46'890
$s = 2004$	0.0014

Table 3.9. monetary yearly renewable terms premium

The reinsurance premium looks rather small compared to the pure risk premium $l_x \cdot \Pi \cdot Z_{t_0}^{(s)}$. This comes from the fact that σ is rather small, that the minimal guarantee $i = 1.5\%$ is rather low compared to the yield $R(t_0, \cdot)$ in year $t_0 = 2000$, and from the fact the randomness of D_x is rather small compared to the total volume l_x.

4

Financial risks

In the previous chapter we have defined the valuation portfolio VaPo for life insurance policies. This valuation portfolio VaPo can be viewed as a replicating portfolio for the insurance liabilities in terms of financial instruments. In this chapter we analyze financial risks which come from the fact that the VaPo and the real existing asset portfolio may differ.

4.1 Asset liability management

We assume that the VaPo and the VaPo^{prot} consist of instruments which can be bought on the asset market (this is reasonable for life insurance). We should now compare this VaPo^{prot} to the **existing asset portfolio** S of our insurance company.

In the sequel we drop the upper index *prot*.

Definition 4.1 *If we buy* VaPo *as assets the resulting portfolio is called Replicating Portfolio* RPo.

It is convenient to use VaPo for both: 1) the portfolio of liabilities protected against technical risks, 2) the replicating portfolio of assets, since they are physically the same portfolio.

Definition 4.2 *Financial risk derives from the fact that the existing asset portfolio S and* VaPo *differ.*

Financial risk management and asset liability management ALM is now concerned with maximizing financial return under the constraint that one has to cover the given liabilities. Goal is to obtain solvency at any time, where solvency is defined relative to an accounting principle.

In the sequel we choose the economic accounting principle $\mathcal{E}$ (see Section 3.3). Here, this corresponds to the prices that are paid at the asset market for the different financial instruments. Since these prices are time dependent,

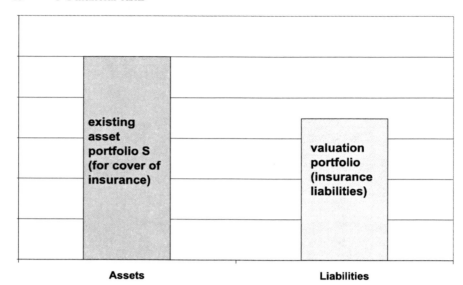

Fig. 4.1. Existing asset portfolio S for the cover of insurance and valuation portfolio protected against technical risks VaPo^{prot}

we attach a subscript t_0 to the accounting principle denoting the time point at which the price of the financial instrument is evaluated. That is, for $t_0 \geq 0$ we denote by $\mathcal{E}_{t_0} = \mathcal{E} \left(\cdot \mid \mathcal{G}_{t_0} \right)$ the accounting principle used at time t_0 (this is simply the continuous positive linear functional used at time t_0 which maps from the multidimensional vector space of financial instruments to monetary values in $\mathbb{R}$, see Sections 3.3 and 3.4).

Definition 4.3 *A company is solvent at time* t_0 *if*

$$\mathcal{E}_{t_0} [S] \geq \mathcal{E}_{t_0} [\text{VaPo}] , \tag{4.1}$$

this is the accounting condition (actual market-consistent balance sheet), and

$$\mathcal{E}_t [S] \geq \mathcal{E}_t [\text{VaPo}] \qquad \text{for all } t > t_0, \tag{4.2}$$

this is the insurance contract condition.

$\square$

Remarks.

- Definition 4.3 is our definition for solvency. Pay attention to the fact that there is not a unique definition for solvency, indeed the solvency rules slightly differ from country to country. Moreover, we could replace the economic accounting principle $\mathcal{E}$ by any other appropriate accounting rule $\mathcal{A}$.
- The accounting condition is necessary but not sufficient for solvency.

- Either there is no technical risk involved (i.e. the valuation portfolio is deterministic with respect to technical risks) or if there is technical risk involved, we consider the valuation portfolio protected against technical risks. Hence in both situations the valuation portfolios are assumed to be deterministic (w.r.t. technical risks), hence (4.2) only considers financial risks. This view will be refined in Chapter 6.
- In many solvency considerations the time interval under consideration is 1. This means that one assumes that the accounting condition is fulfilled and that the insurance contract condition is fulfilled in $[t_0, t_0 + 1]$. After $t_0 + 1$ we iterate this procedure with a new accounting condition at $t_0 + 1$. In the sequel, for the protection against financial risks, we will also take up that position. Then the problem of solvency decouples to one-period problems (that need to be calculated recursively).

Task of financial risk management. If (4.1) is satisfied, how do we need to choose our asset portfolio S such that our company is solvent?

S is a dynamic portfolio, which can be restructured at any time.

a) Prudent solution. Choose S at time t_0 as follows

$$S = \text{VaPo} + F, \tag{4.3}$$

where VaPo is self-financing and F is the free reserve or excess capital which must satisfy $\mathcal{E}_t[F] \geq 0$ for all $t \geq t_0$. Hence solvency is guaranteed which, from a mathematical point of view, shows that solvency is possible.

b) Realistic situation.

- S does not contain VaPo.
- ALM mismatch is often wanted, because taking additional financial risks on the asset side opens the possibility for higher investment returns.
- This mismatch asks for additional protections against financial risks to achieve solvency. In fact regulators ask for a substantially increased target capital for the protection against financial risks. It turns out in the Swiss Solvency Test [SST06] that the financial risk is the dominant term for life insurance companies, whereas in a typical non-life insurance company the target capital for financial risks has about the same size as the target capital for technical risks.

4.2 Procedure to control financial risks

As described above we decouple the solvency problem into one-period problems. For simplicity we only study the first period $[t_0, t_0 + 1]$. We decompose our portfolio at the beginning t_0 of the accounting year into three parts

$$S = \widetilde{S} + M + F, \tag{4.4}$$

where $\widetilde{S}$ is any asset portfolio which satisfies the accounting condition, and M is a margin which is determined below, i.e.

$$\mathcal{E}_{t_0}[\text{VaPo}] = \mathcal{E}_{t_0}\left[\widetilde{S}\right] \quad \text{accounting condition,}$$
$$M \quad\quad\quad\quad\quad\quad \text{margin,} \quad\quad\quad\quad\quad\quad (4.5)$$
$$F \quad\quad\quad\quad\quad\quad \text{free reserves, excess capital.}$$

At the end $t_0 + 1$ of the accounting year (before adding additional insurance contracts to our balance sheet), we should be able to

(1) switch from $\widetilde{S} + M$ to VaPo if necessary,

(2) $\mathcal{E}_t(F)$ is not allowed to become negative.

I.e. the margin M is calculated such that we are able to switch from $\widetilde{S} + M$ to VaPo at the end of the accounting period $[t_0, t_0 + 1]$, if necessary.

Formalizing (1). A Margrabe option is the right to exchange one asset for another. It is named after William Margrabe [Ma78].

Hence, in terms of financial instruments, M is a Margrabe option that allows for switching from the asset portfolio $\widetilde{S}$ to the asset portfolio VaPo whenever

$$\mathcal{E}_{t_0+1}[\text{VaPo}] > \mathcal{E}_{t_0+1}\left[\widetilde{S}\right]. \quad\quad\quad (4.6)$$

Therefore, in order to calculate the price of the Margrabe option, we consider in the sequel the two stochastic price processes generated by $\widetilde{S}$ and VaPo

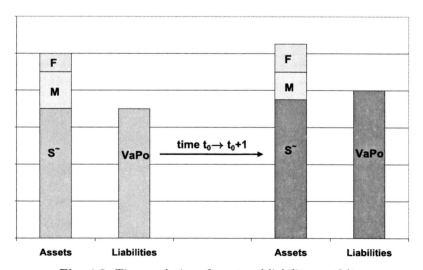

Fig. 4.2. Time evolution of asset and liability portfolios

$$Y_t = \mathcal{E}_t \left[\widetilde{S} \right], \tag{4.7}$$

$$V_t = \mathcal{E}_t \left[\text{VaPo} \right]. \tag{4.8}$$

For explicit calculations it will be useful to consider a continuous time $t \in [t_0, t_0 + 1]$ model because this allows for applying classical financial mathematics like the geometric Brownian motion framework.

4.3 Financial modeling

4.3.1 Stochastic discounting

Consider the deflators $\varphi_t^{(\mathcal{G})}$ for financial variables as defined in an interval $a \le t \le b$. Take any financial instrument or portfolio on the asset market with value A_t at time t.

The asset pricing philosophy (no arbitrage) says that the deflated price process $\varphi_t^{(\mathcal{G})} \cdot A_t$ has at time $s < t$ value (martingale condition, see Section 2.5)

$$E \left[\varphi_t^{(\mathcal{G})} \cdot A_t \,\middle|\, \mathcal{G}_s \right] = \varphi_s^{(\mathcal{G})} \cdot A_s. \tag{4.9}$$

If we denote by $\mathbf{Z}^{(t)}$ the cash flow of the zero coupon bond paying 1 at time t. Then the value $Z_s^{(t)}$ $(s \le t)$ of the zero coupon bond at time s is given by (see (2.44), $Z_t^{(t)} = 1$)

$$Z_s^{(t)} = Q_s \left[\mathbf{Z}^{(t)} \right] = \frac{1}{\varphi_s^{(\mathcal{G})}} \cdot E \left[\varphi_t^{(\mathcal{G})} \,\middle|\, \mathcal{G}_s \right] \tag{4.10}$$

$$= \frac{1}{\varphi_s^{(\mathcal{G})}} \cdot E \left[\varphi_t^{(\mathcal{G})} \cdot Z_t^{(t)} \,\middle|\, \mathcal{G}_s \right] = E \left[\frac{\varphi_t^{(\mathcal{G})}}{\varphi_s^{(\mathcal{G})}} \,\middle|\, \mathcal{G}_s \right].$$

Remarks.

- We have seen in Lemma 2.4 that $\varphi_s^{(\mathcal{G})} \cdot Z_s^{(t)}$ forms an $\mathcal{G}_s$-martingale under P.
- At time 0 we have (see (2.26))

$$Z_0^{(t)} = Q_0 \left[\mathbf{Z}^{(t)} \right] = Q \left[\mathbf{Z}^{(t)} \right] = E[\varphi_t^{(\mathcal{G})}] = D_{0,t}. \tag{4.11}$$

Often one considers transformed probability measures P^* (with the Radon-Nikodym derivative), see Lemma 2.5 in order to get discount factors that are measurable at the beginning of the period under consideration. For example, in view of (2.68) we have for the one-period model

$$A_0 = D_{0,1} \cdot E^* \left[A_1 \right] = E \left[\varphi_1^{(\mathcal{G})} \cdot A_1 \right]. \tag{4.12}$$

4.3.2 Modeling Margrabe options

Recall definitions (4.7)-(4.8). It is often convenient to calculate with

$$\widetilde{Y}_t = \frac{Y_t}{V_t} = \frac{\mathcal{E}_t\left[\widetilde{S}\right]}{\mathcal{E}_t\left[\text{VaPo}\right]}, \tag{4.13}$$

these are the assets measured relative to the liabilities. The advantage of using $\widetilde{Y}_t$ is that the discount disappears, since both expressions have the same time value. Growth of $\widetilde{Y}_t$ means that we have an extensive growth of Y_t (relative to V_t).

In the sequel we identify the solvency problem in $[t_0, t_0 + 1]$ for which we would like to price the Margrabe option exercised at $t_0 + 1$. If we price the Margrabe option at time t_0, we need to model/calculate (see (2.64))

$$Z_{t_0}^{(t_0+1)} \cdot E^*\left[(V_{t_0+1} - Y_{t_0+1})_+ \,\middle|\, \mathcal{G}_{t_0}\right] = E^{**}\left[\left(1 - \widetilde{Y}_{t_0+1}\right)_+ \,\middle|\, \mathcal{G}_{t_0}\right] \cdot V_{t_0}, \tag{4.14}$$

where the transformed measure is defined by

$$dP^{**}(\cdot|\mathcal{G}_{t_0}) = Z_{t_0}^{(t_0+1)} \cdot \frac{V_{t_0+1}}{V_{t_0}} \cdot dP^*(\cdot|\mathcal{G}_{t_0}). \tag{4.15}$$

Observe that

$$E^{**}\left[1|\mathcal{G}_{t_0}\right] = E^*\left[Z_{t_0}^{(t_0+1)} \cdot \frac{V_{t_0+1}}{V_{t_0}} \,\middle|\, \mathcal{G}_{t_0}\right] = 1, \tag{4.16}$$

due to the martingale property of discounted price processes w.r.t. P^*. Hence from the right-hand side of (4.14) we need to model

$$V_{t_0} \cdot E^{**}\left[\left(1 - \widetilde{Y}_{t_0+1}\right)_+ \,\middle|\, \mathcal{G}_{t_0}\right], \tag{4.17}$$

where prices are relative to the initial value $V_{t_0} = \mathcal{E}_{t_0}(\text{VaPo})$ of the valuation portfolio.

Example 4.1.

We assume that $\widetilde{Y}_t = \exp\{W_t\} \sim \widetilde{P}$ follows a geometric Brownian motion, with $(W_t)_{t_0 \leq t \leq t_0+1}$ is a one-dimensional Wiener process with mean $\mu(t - t_0)$ and variance $\sigma^2(t - t_0)$, i.e. $W_t \sim \mathcal{N}(\mu(t - t_0), \sigma^2(t - t_0))$. The equivalent martingale measure P^{**} is given by eliminating the drift part, $W_t \sim \mathcal{N}(-\sigma^2/2(t-t_0), \sigma^2(t-t_0))$ (see also (3.59)), hence (4.17) is simply the price of a European put option which can be derived from the Black-Scholes formula (see e.g. [LL91], Section 3.2):

$$E^{**}\left[\left(1 - \widetilde{Y}_{t_0+1}\right)_+ \,\middle|\, \mathcal{G}_{t_0}\right] = \Phi(\sigma/2) - \Phi(-\sigma/2), \tag{4.18}$$

where $\Phi(\cdot)$ denotes the standard Gaussian distribution.

We find the following relative loadings (depending on the volatility of the assets relative to the liabilities):

σ	price relative to V_{t_0}
0.05	1.99%
0.10	3.99%
0.20	7.97%
0.30	11.92%

□

4.3.3 Conclusions

We have decoupled the solvency problem into recursive one-period problems. To protect against financial risks one has to spend each year the price of the Margrabe option. This price measures the ALM mismatch between the real asset portfolio $\widetilde{S}$ and the liability portfolio VaPo.

The agents who are entitled to receive the earnings beyond the VaPo should also finance this option:

- With profit policy share the price: Between the policyholder and the shareholder according to their participation.
- Non-participating policy: Shareholder has to pay the full price.

As the price of the Margrabe option is relative to the VaPo, we can easily do the similar calculation for the VaPo protected against technical risks. And if the VaPo protected against technical risks can not be financed we need to a) have more capital, b) do better ALM, and/or c) reduce technical risks.

4.4 Pricing Margrabe options

The VaPo protected against financial risks will provide us each year with the price of a Margrabe option, which can be used to

1. buy the option (often not realistic),
2. hedge the option,
3. cover the cost of risk bearing capital RBC.

This section is an excursion to financial mathematics. We describe the pricing and hedging of Margrabe options. In order to do so, we switch to a continuous time framework. We decribe pricing of financial instruments using Esscher transforms which are well-known in actuarial mathematics.

4.4.1 Pricing using Esscher transforms

To derive the price of a Margrabe option we closely follow Gerber-Shiu [GS94b].

Choose $\delta > 0$ and $t \geq 0$. We assume that our financial market consists of L financial assets. Assume that $A_1(t), \ldots, A_L(t) > 0$ denote the price processes of the L non-dividend paying assets at time t. We define the logarithmized price process

$$B_i(t) = \log\left(\frac{A_i(t)}{A_i(0)}\right) \in \mathbb{R}, \tag{4.19}$$

for $i = 1, \ldots, L$ and $t \geq 0$. Moreover

$$\mathbf{B}(t) = (B_1(t), \ldots, B_L(t))^T, \tag{4.20}$$

is a stochastic vector in $\mathbb{R}^L$ with distribution

$$F(\mathbf{x}, t) = P[B_i(t) \leq x_i, i = 1, \ldots, L] \tag{4.21}$$

for all $t \geq 0$ and $\mathbf{x} \in \mathbb{R}^L$.

We define the moment generating function as follows, for $\mathbf{z} \in \mathbb{R}^L$ and $t \geq 0$

$$M(\mathbf{z}, t) = E\left[\exp\left\{\mathbf{z}^T \cdot \mathbf{B}(t)\right\}\right]. \tag{4.22}$$

Assumptions. Assume that the stochastic process $\{\mathbf{B}(t)\}_{t \geq 0}$ has stationary, independent increments and that

$$M(\mathbf{z}, t) = [M(\mathbf{z}, 1)]^t. \tag{4.23}$$

Moreover, we assume that $\mathbf{B}(t)$ has a density for $t \geq 0$:

$$f(\mathbf{x}, t) = \frac{\partial^L}{\partial x_1 \cdots \partial x_L} F(\mathbf{x}, t). \tag{4.24}$$

$\square$

The modified density under the Esscher transform is for $\mathbf{h} \in \mathbb{R}^L$ defined as follows:

$$f(\mathbf{x}, t; \mathbf{h}) = \frac{\exp\left\{\mathbf{h}^T \cdot \mathbf{x}\right\} \cdot f(\mathbf{x}, t)}{M(\mathbf{h}, t)}, \tag{4.25}$$

the corresponding moment generating function is given by

$$M(\mathbf{z}, t; \mathbf{h}) = \frac{M(\mathbf{z} + \mathbf{h}, t)}{M(\mathbf{h}, t)}. \tag{4.26}$$

Define the transformed distribution: $F_{\mathbf{h}}(\cdot, \cdot) = F(\cdot, \cdot; \mathbf{h})$, where $F(\cdot, \cdot; \mathbf{h})$ denotes the distribution to the density $f(\cdot, \cdot; \mathbf{h})$. Then the Esscher transform of the process $\{\mathbf{B}(t)\}_{t \geq 0}$ has again stationary, independent increments with

$$M(\mathbf{z}, t; \mathbf{h}) = [M(\mathbf{z}, 1; \mathbf{h})]^t. \tag{4.27}$$

Our goal is to choose $\mathbf{h}^* \in \mathbb{R}^L$ such that the processes

$$\left\{ e^{-\delta t} A_i(t) \right\}_{t \geq 0} \tag{4.28}$$

are martingales w.r.t. $F^* = F_{\mathbf{h}^*}(\cdot, \cdot) = F(\cdot, \cdot; \mathbf{h}^*)$ and $(\mathcal{G}_t)_t$:
Choose $s \in [0, t]$ then

$$
\begin{aligned}
E^* \left[e^{-\delta t} A_i(t) \middle| \mathcal{G}_s \right] &= e^{-\delta t} \cdot A_i(0) \cdot E^* \left[\exp \{ B_i(t) \} \middle| \mathcal{G}_s \right] \\
&= e^{-\delta t} \cdot A_i(0) \cdot E^* \left[\exp \{ B_i(t) - B_i(s) + B_i(s) \} \middle| \mathcal{G}_s \right] \\
&= e^{-\delta t} \cdot A_i(0) \cdot \exp \{ B_i(s) \} \cdot E^* \left[\exp \{ B_i(t) - B_i(s) \} \middle| \mathcal{G}_s \right] \\
&= e^{-\delta s} \cdot A_i(s) \cdot e^{-\delta(t-s)} \cdot E^* \left[\exp \{ B_i(t) - B_i(s) \} \middle| \mathcal{G}_s \right].
\end{aligned}
\tag{4.29}
$$

Since we have stationary, independent increments, $\mathbf{h}^* \in \mathbb{R}^L$ must satisfy for all $s \leq t$

$$E^* \left[\exp \{ B_i(t) - B_i(s) \} \middle| \mathcal{G}_s \right] = E^* \left[\exp \{ B_i(t-s) \} \right] = e^{\delta(t-s)}. \tag{4.30}$$

This implies that

$$
\begin{aligned}
e^{\delta(t-s)} &= E^* \left[\exp \{ B_i(t-s) \} \right] \\
&= E_{\mathbf{h}^*} \left[\exp \{ B_i(t-s) \} \right] \\
&= M(\mathbf{1}_i, t-s; \mathbf{h}^*) = [M(\mathbf{1}_i, 1; \mathbf{h}^*)]^{t-s},
\end{aligned}
\tag{4.31}
$$

where $\mathbf{1}_i = (0, \ldots, 0, 1, 0, \ldots, 0)^T \in \mathbb{R}^L$. But this immediately implies that

$$e^{\delta} = M(\mathbf{1}_i, 1; \mathbf{h}^*). \tag{4.32}$$

It can be shown (see Gerber-Shiu [GS94a]) that there is a unique solution $\mathbf{h}^* \in \mathbb{R}^L$, which satisfies (4.32) for all $i = 1, \ldots, L$. Hence we have found an equivalent martingale measure for the discounted price processes.

Remarks.

- The parameter $\mathbf{h}^*$ is called the risk-neutral Esscher transform parameter and the corresponding equivalent martingale measure $F^* = F_{\mathbf{h}^*}(\cdot, \cdot) = F(\cdot, \cdot; \mathbf{h}^*)$ the risk-neutral Esscher measure.
- Since $\mathbf{h}^*$ is unique we have that the risk-neutral Esscher measure is unique. However, there may be other equivalent martingale measures, i.e. the market is not necessarily complete.

Theorem 4.4 *Let* $g : \mathbb{R}^L \to \mathbb{R}$ *be a measurable function. Then for all* $t > 0$ *we have the following identity*

$$E_{\mathbf{h}^*} \left[e^{-\delta t} A_i(t) \cdot g \left(A_1(t), \ldots, A_n(t) \right) \right] = A_i(0) \cdot E_{\mathbf{h}^* + \mathbf{1}_i} \left[g \left(A_1(t), \ldots, A_n(t) \right) \right]. \tag{4.33}$$

Proof. We consider

$$e^{x_i} \cdot f(\mathbf{x}, t; \mathbf{h}^*) = e^{\mathbf{x}^T \cdot \mathbf{1}_i} \cdot f(\mathbf{x}, t; \mathbf{h}^*) \tag{4.34}$$
$$= \frac{e^{\mathbf{x}^T \cdot (\mathbf{h}^* + \mathbf{1}_i)} \cdot f(\mathbf{x}, t)}{M(\mathbf{h}^*, t)}$$
$$= f(\mathbf{x}, t; \mathbf{h}^* + \mathbf{1}_i) \cdot \frac{M(\mathbf{h}^* + \mathbf{1}_i, t)}{M(\mathbf{h}^*, t)}$$
$$= f(\mathbf{x}, t; \mathbf{h}^* + \mathbf{1}_i) \cdot M(\mathbf{1}_i, t; \mathbf{h}^*).$$

By the choice of $\mathbf{h}^*$ this last expression is equal to

$$e^{x_i} \cdot f(\mathbf{x}, t; \mathbf{h}^*) = e^{\delta t} \cdot f(\mathbf{x}, t; \mathbf{h}^* + \mathbf{1}_i). \tag{4.35}$$

But this immediately implies that

$$E_{\mathbf{h}^*} \left[e^{-\delta t} A_i(t) \cdot g\left(A_1(t), \ldots, A_n(t)\right) \right] \tag{4.36}$$
$$= A_i(0) \cdot E_{\mathbf{h}^*} \left[e^{-\delta t} \cdot e^{B_i(t)} \cdot g\left(A_1(t), \ldots, A_n(t)\right) \right]$$
$$= A_i(0) \cdot E_{\mathbf{h}^* + \mathbf{1}_i} \left[g\left(A_1(t), \ldots, A_n(t)\right) \right],$$

which finishes the proof.

$\square$

This gives us the following corollary for the Esscher price of the Margrabe option

Corollary 4.5 (Margrabe Option) *Assume $L = 2$. The Esscher value at time 0 of an option to exchange $A_2(t)$ for $A_1(t)$ at time $t > 0$ is*

$$A_1(0) \cdot P_{\mathbf{h}^* + \mathbf{1}_1} \left[A_1(t) > A_2(t) \right] - A_2(0) \cdot P_{\mathbf{h}^* + \mathbf{1}_2} \left[A_1(t) > A_2(t) \right]. \tag{4.37}$$

Proof. The value of the option at time 0 is

$$E_{\mathbf{h}^*} \left[e^{-\delta t} \cdot (A_1(t) - A_2(t))_+ \right] \tag{4.38}$$
$$= E_{\mathbf{h}^*} \left[e^{-\delta t} \cdot (A_1(t) - A_2(t)) \cdot 1_{\{A_1(t) > A_2(t)\}} \right]$$
$$= E_{\mathbf{h}^*} \left[e^{-\delta t} \cdot A_1(t) \cdot 1_{\{A_1(t) > A_2(t)\}} \right] - E_{\mathbf{h}^*} \left[e^{-\delta t} \cdot A_2(t) \cdot 1_{\{A_1(t) > A_2(t)\}} \right]$$
$$= A_1(0) \cdot E_{\mathbf{h}^* + \mathbf{1}_1} \left[1_{\{A_1(t) > A_2(t)\}} \right] - A_2(0) \cdot E_{\mathbf{h}^* + \mathbf{1}_2} \left[1_{\{A_1(t) > A_2(t)\}} \right].$$

This finishes the proof of the corollary.

$\square$

Remark. Theorem 4.4 can also be used to price a European call option with strike K at time τ: Assume that $A_1(t)$ is the price process of the underlying asset and define $A_2(t) = K \cdot e^{\delta(t-\tau)}$. Then the Esscher price of the European call can be calculated from Theorem 4.4 using the function $g(x_1, x_2) = (x_1 - x_2)_+$.

4.4.2 Application of the Esscher transform to the multi-dimensional Wiener process

We now choose a specific underlying price process $\mathbf{A}(t)$. Assume that $\mathbf{B}(t) = \log(\mathbf{A}(t)/\mathbf{A}(0))$ is a multidimensional Wiener process with non-singular covariance matrix Σ and mean $\boldsymbol{\mu} \in \mathbb{R}^L$ (see (4.19)-(4.20)). That is, $\mathbf{B}(t)$ has density

$$f(\mathbf{x}, t) = \frac{1}{(2\pi)^{L/2} \cdot |t\Sigma|^{1/2}} \cdot \exp\left\{-(\mathbf{x} - t\boldsymbol{\mu})^T (2t\Sigma)^{-1}(\mathbf{x} - t\boldsymbol{\mu})\right\}. \quad (4.39)$$

The moment generating function is then given by ($\mathbf{z} \in \mathbb{R}^L$)

$$M(\mathbf{z}, t) = E\left[\exp\left\{\mathbf{z} \cdot \mathbf{B}(t)\right\}\right] = \exp\left\{t \cdot \left[\mathbf{z}^T \boldsymbol{\mu} + 1/2 \cdot \mathbf{z}^T \Sigma \mathbf{z}\right]\right\}, \quad (4.40)$$

and for $\mathbf{h} \in \mathbb{R}^L$

$$\begin{aligned}
M(\mathbf{z}, t; \mathbf{h}) &= \frac{M(\mathbf{z} + \mathbf{h}, t)}{M(\mathbf{h}, t)} \quad &(4.41) \\
&= \exp\left\{t \cdot \left[(\mathbf{z} + \mathbf{h})^T \boldsymbol{\mu} + 1/2 \cdot (\mathbf{z} + \mathbf{h})^T \Sigma (\mathbf{z} + \mathbf{h})\right]\right\} \\
&\quad \cdot \exp\left\{-t \cdot \left[\mathbf{h}^T \boldsymbol{\mu} + 1/2 \cdot \mathbf{h}^T \Sigma \mathbf{h}\right]\right\} \\
&= \exp\left\{t \cdot \left[\mathbf{z}^T \cdot (\boldsymbol{\mu} + \Sigma \mathbf{h}) + 1/2 \cdot \mathbf{z}^T \Sigma \mathbf{z}\right]\right\}.
\end{aligned}$$

Henceforth, the Esscher transform of an L-dimensional Wiener process is again an L-dimensional Wiener process with modified mean vector $\boldsymbol{\mu} \mapsto \boldsymbol{\mu} + \Sigma \mathbf{h}$ and unchanged covariance matrix Σ.

Equation (4.32) implies that for all $i = 1, \ldots, L$

$$\delta = \mathbf{1}_i^T \cdot (\boldsymbol{\mu} + \Sigma \mathbf{h}^*) + 1/2 \cdot \mathbf{1}_i^T \Sigma \mathbf{1}_i, \quad (4.42)$$

which gives us, $\Sigma = (\sigma_{i,j})_{i,j}$,

$$\boldsymbol{\mu} + \Sigma \mathbf{h}^* = \left(\delta - \sigma_{1,1}/2, \ldots, \delta - \sigma_{L,L}/2\right), \quad (4.43)$$
$$\boldsymbol{\mu} + \Sigma(\mathbf{h}^* + \mathbf{1}_i) = \left(\delta + \sigma_{1,i} - \sigma_{1,1}/2, \ldots, \delta + \sigma_{L,i} - \sigma_{L,L}/2\right). \quad (4.44)$$

Note that the right-hand side of (4.43)-(4.44) is independent of $\boldsymbol{\mu}$.

If we apply Corollary 4.5 to the 2-dimensional Wiener process $\mathbf{B}(t) = (B_1(t), B_2(t))$, we obtain

$$\begin{aligned}
E_{\mathbf{h}^*}&\left[e^{-\delta t} \cdot (A_1(t) - A_2(t))_+\right] \quad &(4.45) \\
&= A_1(0) \cdot P_{\mathbf{h}^* + \mathbf{1}_1}\left[A_1(t) > A_2(t)\right] - A_2(0) \cdot P_{\mathbf{h}^* + \mathbf{1}_2}\left[A_1(t) > A_2(t)\right] \\
&= A_1(0) \cdot P_{\mathbf{h}^* + \mathbf{1}_1}\left[W(t) < \zeta\right] - A_2(0) \cdot P_{\mathbf{h}^* + \mathbf{1}_2}\left[W(t) < \zeta\right],
\end{aligned}$$

with $\zeta = \log(A_1(0)/A_2(0))$ and $W(t) = B_2(t) - B_1(t)$. $W(1)$ has the following distributions

$$\mathcal{N}\left(-\sigma_{1,1}/2 + \sigma_{2,1} - \sigma_{2,2}/2, \sigma_{1,1} - 2\sigma_{1,2} + \sigma_{2,2}\right) \quad \text{under } P_{\mathbf{h}^*+\mathbf{1}_1}, \quad (4.46)$$
$$\mathcal{N}\left(\sigma_{1,1}/2 - \sigma_{2,1} + \sigma_{2,2}/2, \sigma_{1,1} - 2\sigma_{1,2} + \sigma_{2,2}\right) \quad \text{under } P_{\mathbf{h}^*+\mathbf{1}_2}. \quad (4.47)$$

With $\mathcal{N}(\mu, \sigma^2)$ we denote the one-dimensional Gaussian distribution with mean μ and variance σ^2, $\Phi(\cdot)$ denotes the standard Gaussian distribution ($\mu = 0$ and $\sigma^2 = 1$) and φ its density.

Let us define

$$v^2 = \sigma_{1,1} - 2\sigma_{1,2} + \sigma_{2,2} = \sigma_1^2 - 2\rho\sigma_1\sigma_2 + \sigma_2^2, \quad (4.48)$$

with $\sigma_1^2 = \sigma_{1,1}$, $\sigma_2^2 = \sigma_{2,2}$ and $\rho = \sigma_{1,2}/(\sigma_1\sigma_2)$. Then we see that $W(t)$ has the following distributions

$$\mathcal{N}\left(-v^2 t/2, tv^2\right) \quad \text{under } P_{\mathbf{h}^*+\mathbf{1}_1}, \quad (4.49)$$
$$\mathcal{N}\left(v^2 t/2, tv^2\right) \quad \text{under } P_{\mathbf{h}^*+\mathbf{1}_2}. \quad (4.50)$$

So we immediately have the next corollary, which gives the value of the Margrabe option for a 2-dimensional Wiener process:

Corollary 4.6 (Margrabe Option for Wiener process)

$$E_{\mathbf{h}^*}\left[e^{-\delta t} \cdot (A_1(t) - A_2(t))_+\right] \quad (4.51)$$
$$= A_1(0) \cdot \Phi\left(\frac{\zeta + v^2 t/2}{vt^{1/2}}\right) - A_2(0) \cdot \Phi\left(\frac{\zeta - v^2 t/2}{vt^{1/2}}\right).$$

If we come back to (4.4): We define the price process of the Margrabe option by M_t, $t \in [t_0, t_0 + 1]$, to exchange $\tilde{S}$ by the valuation portfolio VaPo at time $t_0 + 1$. We choose

$$A_1(t) = V_t = \mathcal{E}_t\left[\text{VaPo}\right] \quad \text{and} \quad A_2(t) = Y_t = \mathcal{E}_t\left[\tilde{S}\right], \quad (4.52)$$

then

$$\zeta_t = \log\left(\frac{A_1(t)}{A_2(t)}\right) = \log\left(\frac{V_t}{Y_t}\right) = -\log \tilde{Y}_t. \quad (4.53)$$

Hence the price process of the Margrabe option is given by (see Corollary 4.6)

$$M_t = V_t \cdot \left[\Phi\left(\frac{\zeta_t + v_t^2/2}{v_t}\right) - e^{-\zeta_t} \cdot \Phi\left(\frac{\zeta_t - v_t^2/2}{v_t}\right)\right] \quad (4.54)$$
$$= Y_t \cdot \left[e^{\zeta_t} \cdot \Phi\left(\frac{\zeta_t + v_t^2/2}{v_t}\right) - \Phi\left(\frac{\zeta_t - v_t^2/2}{v_t}\right)\right],$$

where $v_t^2 = v^2 \cdot (t_0 + 1 - t)$, which implies at $t = t_0$

$$M_{t_0} = V_{t_0} \cdot \left[\Phi\left(v/2\right) - \Phi\left(-v/2\right)\right], \quad (4.55)$$

see also (4.18).

4.4.3 Hedging Margrabe options

We have seen that the price process of the Margrabe option M_t for 2-dimensional Wiener processes is given by (4.54). We consider now the price process $Y_t + M_t$ which allows for switching from $\tilde{S}$ to VaPo in $t \in [t_0, t_0 + 1]$. Since in practice, we are not able to buy such a Margrabe option, we need to use a hedging strategy to protect ourselves against financial losses.

Define the function

$$H(t,x) = x \cdot \Phi\left(\frac{\log x + v_t^2/2}{v_t}\right) - \Phi\left(\frac{\log x - v_t^2/2}{v_t}\right). \tag{4.56}$$

Then we have

$$M_t = Y_t \cdot H(t, e^{\zeta_t}) = Y_t \cdot H\left(t, \tilde{Y}_t^{-1}\right) \tag{4.57}$$

and with Itô calculus one sees that we have to study

$$\frac{\partial}{\partial x} H(t,x) \tag{4.58}$$

$$= \Phi\left(\frac{\log x + v_t^2/2}{v_t}\right) + \varphi\left(\frac{\log x + v_t^2/2}{v_t}\right)/v_t - \varphi\left(\frac{\log x - v_t^2/2}{v_t}\right)/(xv_t)$$

$$= \Phi\left(\frac{\log x + v_t^2/2}{v_t}\right),$$

which is a well-known expression for the European call option in the Black-Scholes model (see e.g. Remarque 3.6 in [LL91] on p. 79).

Hence for the hedging strategy $\psi = (\tilde{\lambda}_t, \lambda_t)$ we obtain the following natural candidate (see e.g. Section 3.3 in [LL91]): Invest

$$\tilde{\lambda}_t = \left.\frac{\partial}{\partial x} H(t,x)\right|_{x = e^{\zeta_t} = \tilde{Y}_t^{-1}} = \Phi\left(\frac{\zeta_t + v_t^2/2}{v_t}\right) \tag{4.59}$$

into the asset V_t and

$$\lambda_t = 1 - \Phi\left(\frac{\zeta_t - v_t^2/2}{v_t}\right) \tag{4.60}$$

into asset Y_t.

Hence the value of our portfolio is at any time t

$$\tilde{\lambda}_t \cdot V_t + \lambda_t \cdot Y_t = V_t \cdot \left[\tilde{\lambda}_t + e^{-\zeta_t} \cdot \lambda_t\right] \tag{4.61}$$

$$= V_t \cdot \left[\Phi\left(\frac{\zeta_t + v_t^2/2}{v_t}\right) + e^{-\zeta_t} \cdot \left(1 - \Phi\left(\frac{\zeta_t - v_t^2/2}{v_t}\right)\right)\right]$$

$$= e^{-\zeta_t} \cdot V_t + M_t = Y_t + M_t,$$

which means that we can switch to the VaPo at any time t.

Remark. The choice (4.59) is done since it reflects the relative change of the value of the Margrabe option as a function of time.

Example 4.2.

v	0.05					

Y~=Y/V	lambda*Y	lambda~*V	M+Y	lambda units of Y	lambda units of V
1.0000	51.0%	51.0%	102.00%	51.0%	51.0%
1.0077	51.4%	51.0%	102.39%	57.3%	44.6%
1.0215	58.5%	44.6%	103.12%	68.8%	32.9%
1.0295	70.8%	32.9%	103.66%	75.6%	25.8%
1.0100	76.3%	25.8%	102.13%	60.4%	41.2%
1.0423	63.0%	41.2%	104.14%	86.5%	14.3%
1.0443	90.4%	14.3%	104.68%	89.3%	11.3%
1.0192	91.0%	11.3%	102.38%	72.8%	28.3%
1.0252	74.6%	28.3%	102.92%	81.0%	19.8%
1.0062	81.5%	19.8%	101.30%	60.2%	40.7%
0.9901	59.7%	40.7%	100.37%	31.7%	69.1%
0.9941	31.5%	69.1%	100.54%	34.4%	66.2%
0.9845	33.8%	66.2%	100.00%	0.0%	100.0%

Fig. 4.3. One realization of $\widetilde{Y}_t$ with its associated value process $M_t + Y_t$

We choose $v = 0.05$ as in Example 4.1. This immediately implies that the price of the Margrabe option is $M_{t_0} = 2\% \cdot V_{t_0}$. This leads for a specific realization of $\widetilde{Y}_t$ to the following development of the price process: see Figure 4.3.

If we plot the process for three different realizations of the $\widetilde{Y}_t$ we obtain a picture as shown in Figure 4.4.

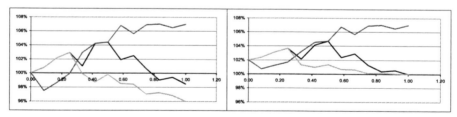

Fig. 4.4. We have plotted three different realizations of $\widetilde{Y}$ and the corresponding value processes $M_t + Y_t$

Observe that the path of $M_t + Y_t$ never falls below V_t, i.e. we have full financial coverage of all liabilities during the whole investment period.

□

Conclusions. If we can not buy the Margrabe option we need to hedge for switching into the VaPo at the end of each year.

The hedging strategy can be made cheaper, if we only hedge for switching at the point when the money is needed → the price of the Margrabe option becomes cheaper.

(a) Money is needed in n years. Switch at the end of every year. Henceforth, the price is

$$n \cdot \text{ price Margrabe option}(\sigma). \tag{4.62}$$

(b) Money is needed in n years. Switch at the end of the period. Henceforth, the price is

$$\text{price Margrabe option}(\sqrt{n} \cdot \sigma) \sim \sqrt{n} \cdot \text{ price Margrabe option}(\sigma). \tag{4.63}$$

4.4.4 Risk bearing capital

We can also use the price of the Margrabe option to cover the costs of risk bearing capital. If our risk measure is Value-at-Risk, we choose q_{t_0} such that for given small $\varepsilon > 0$

$$\widetilde{P}\left[(1 + q_{t_0})\,\widetilde{Y}_{t_0+1} \geq 1 \Big| \mathcal{G}_{t_0}\right] \geq 1 - \varepsilon, \tag{4.64}$$

i.e. only with small probability (ε) we have a short-fall which can not be financed by the risk bearing capital.

From the theoretical point of view, this is not an ideal solution, but it is the solution, which is (at the moment) applied in many practical solvency applications like the Swiss Solvency Test [SST06].

Under the simple standard model from last section (Wiener process), we obtain

$$\widetilde{P}\left[\log \widetilde{Y}_{t_0+1} \geq -\log(1 + q_{t_0}) \Big| \mathcal{G}_{t_0}\right] = 1 - \varepsilon. \tag{4.65}$$

Henceforth q_{t_0} is given by ($\sigma = v$)

$$-\log(1 + q_{t_0}) = \sigma \cdot \Phi^{-1}(\varepsilon) + \mu. \tag{4.66}$$

Example 4.3.

We choose the following example: assume that we can choose our default probability ε. For example, Standard & Poors gives ratings for the choosen default probabilities. The result is shown in Figure 4.5.

Observe that for the risk bearing capital we also need to specify the expected return μ. In discussions with economists and in the developments of the Swiss Solvency Test it has turned out that it is highly non-trivial to estimate μ for the different asset classes. For example, for the Swiss Solvency Test 2005, even experts have had so different opinions about predictions of μ that at the end one has put the expected investment return equal to the risk-free rate. But Example 4.3 shows that for risk bearing capital it only makes sense to consider the expected return and the expected volatility simultaneously. Higher expected returns will increase the volatility. This example also shows that the choice of the asset portfolio is more crucial than the choice of the security level ε.

□

Standard & Poors

Rating	default prob.	normal quantile	sigma mu	0.05 0.012	0.1 0.024	0.15 0.036	0.2 0.048
AAA	0.01%	-3.72		19.0%	41.6%	68.5%	100.5%
AA	0.03%	-3.43		17.3%	37.6%	61.4%	89.3%
A	0.07%	-3.19		15.9%	34.4%	55.8%	80.6%
BBB	0.18%	-2.91		14.3%	30.6%	49.3%	70.6%
BB	1.08%	-2.30		10.8%	22.8%	36.2%	50.9%
B	6.41%	-1.52		6.6%	13.7%	21.2%	29.2%
B-	11.61%	-1.19		4.9%	10.0%	15.4%	21.0%

Price Margrabe Option				2.0%	4.0%	6.0%	8.0%

Fig. 4.5. Risk bearing capital

5

Valuation portfolio in non-life insurance

5.1 Introduction

To illustrate the problem we assume that we have a non-life insurance contract, which protects the policyholder against claims within one calender year. Assume that we receive a premium Π at the beginning of a calender year. Hence the policyholder exchanges the premium Π against a contract, which gives him a cover against well-specified random events (claims) occuring within a fixed time period.

Assume that we have a claim within this fixed time period. In that case the insurance company will replace the financial damage caused by the claim (according to the insurance contract).

In general, the insurance company is not able to assess the claim immediately at the occurence date due to:

1. Usually, there is a reporting delay (time gap between claim occurence and claim reporting to the insurance company). This time gap can be small (a few days), for example, in motor hull insurance, but it can also be quite large (months or years). Especially, in general liability insurance we can have large reporting delays: typical examples are asbestos claims that were caused several years ago but are only noticed and reported today.
2. Usually it takes quite some time to settle a claim (time difference between reporting date and settlement date). This is due to several different reasons, for example, for bodily injury claims we first have to observe the recovery process before finally deciding on the claim and on the compensation, or other claims can only be settled at court which usually takes quite some time until the final settlement. In most cases a (more complex) claim is settled by several payments X_i $(i \geq 1)$: Whenever a bill for that specific claim comes in it is paid by the insurance company.

Assume that a contract (or a portfolio of contracts) generates a cash flow

$$\mathbf{X} = (X_0, \ldots, X_N), \tag{5.1}$$

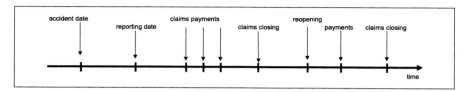

Fig. 5.1. Claims development process

where X_k denotes the payments at time/in period $k \in \mathbb{N}$ ($X_k = 0$ if there is no payment at time k), and N is the (random) number of payments, i.e. the last payment takes place at time/in period N.

We set

$$X_0 = -\Pi, \qquad \text{premium paid at the beginning,} \qquad (5.2)$$

$$X_k, \quad k \geq 1, \qquad \text{nominal claims payments in period } k. \qquad (5.3)$$

We denote cumulative nominal claims payments until time k by

$$C_k = \sum_{j=1}^{k} X_j, \qquad (5.4)$$

henceforth the ultimate loss is given by C_N.

Problems in practice.

(1) Predict C_N for given information $\mathcal{F}_k$ at time k. This is in general a very difficult problem, which is known under the name "claims reserving problem". It is not further discussed here, but there is a vast literature on the claims reserving problem (see e.g. Taylor [Ta00] and the references therein).

(2) Split the total ultimate claim C_N into the different (annual) payments $X_1, \ldots, X_N$, i.e. estimate a payout/cash flow pattern for C_N.

A first idea is to directly predict the X_i. But long time experience indicates that this approach does in most cases not lead to reasonable estimates and predictions for the total claim amount C_N. Therefore one usually proceeds by (1) and then (2), as above. Usually, the following information is used for these predictions:

For (1) paid claims experience, incurred claims experience, claims handling directives, financial parameters, other external knowledge;

For (2) paid claims experience to split C_N into the different periods.

In this lecture we restrict ourselves to *paid claims* data also for (1). In practice, of course, we would also take into account other additional information. This means that in this lecture we assume that the technical information $\mathcal{T}$ is generated by the payments $\mathbf{X}$.

To construct the VaPo in non-life insurance we proceed as in Chapter 3 in two steps:

Step 1. Choose an appropriate basis $\mathcal{U}_1, \mathcal{U}_2, \ldots$ of financial instruments:

- zero coupon bonds $Z^{(t)}$ paying 1 at time t, or
- inflation protected zero coupon bonds,
- etc.

Step 2. Determine the number of units $\Lambda_i(\mathbf{X}_k)$ and $l_{i,k}$, respectively, we need to reserve in order to meet all our future obligations (which are covered by past premium).

Questions: How should we determine our future liabilities of old contracts? We are at time t: How should we reserve? How should we construct the VaPo?

Assumption 5.1

We assume that the appropriate basis are the zero coupon bonds $Z^{(t)}$, i.e. we assume that the price processes of the zero coupon bonds (which generate in our case the financial information $\mathcal{G}$) are independent of the random cash flows $\mathbf{X}$ (which generate in our case the technical information $\mathcal{T}$).

$\square$

For a comment on Assumption 5.1 we refer to Remark 5.2.

(Random) cash flow after time t.

period	instrument	cash flow		units
$t+1$	$Z^{(t+1)}$	X_{t+1}	$\longrightarrow$	$l_{t+1}^{(t)}$
$t+2$	$Z^{(t+2)}$	X_{t+2}	$\longrightarrow$	$l_{t+2}^{(t)}$
$\vdots$	$\vdots$	$\vdots$		$\vdots$
$t+k$	$Z^{(t+k)}$	X_{t+k}	$\longrightarrow$	$l_{t+k}^{(t)}$
$\vdots$	$\vdots$	$\vdots$		$\vdots$

Task: Replace the stochastic cash flows X_{t+k} by deterministic numbers $l_{t+k}^{(t)}$ (where the upper index denotes the information that was used to determine the number of units). In the notation of Chapter 3 we denote the units as follows

$$\mathcal{U}_i = Z^{(t+i)}, \quad i \geq 1. \tag{5.5}$$

Then the number of units $\mathcal{U}_i$ at time t are given by (VaPo without protection against technical risks)

$$\sum_{k \geq 1} l_{i,k}^{(t)} = \sum_{k \geq 1} E\left[\Lambda_i(\mathbf{X}_k)|\mathcal{T}_t\right] = E\left[\Lambda_i(\mathbf{X}_i)|\mathcal{T}_t\right] = l_{i,i}^{(t)}. \tag{5.6}$$

Hence we use the following abbreviations

$$l_i = l_i^{(t)} = l_{i,i}^{(t)} \qquad \text{and} \qquad l_i^* = l_i^{*,t} = l_{i,i}^{*,t}, \qquad (5.7)$$

where l_i^* is the number of units used for the valuation portfolio protected against technical risks. Below we give an explicit construction for the choice of l_i and l_i^*.

Using our Assumption 5.1 we see that

$$l_i = E\left[\Lambda_i(\mathbf{X}_i)|\mathcal{T}_t\right] = E\left[X_i|\mathcal{T}_t\right], \qquad (5.8)$$

where $\mathcal{T}_t = \sigma\{X_0, \dots, X_t\}$.

Remark 5.2

- The financial instruments $Z^{(t+k)}$ are the basis, which represent our cash flow, valuation portfolio respectively. The choice of the basis was rather obvious in life insurance. In non-life insurance this is one of the crucial, non-trivial steps: find a decoupling such that the price process of the units $\mathcal{U}_i$ and the number of units are independent.

  Indeed, the nominal payments X_i depend on the job market, on the financial market, etc. (but also on the line of business we have chosen). Therefore we would need an inflation protected zero coupon bond which reflects what kind of business we write, and how this business is correlated with the financial market (immunization against financial risks).
- In the transformation $X_{t+k} \mapsto l_{t+k}$ we must incorporate a protection/margin for technical risks, hence as in the life chapter we look for l_{t+k}^*. This exactly describes against which shortfalls the insurance company provides protection.
- The transformation $X_{t+k} \mapsto l_{t+k}$ should also incorporate the actual information considered, hence as in (3.51)-(3.52), $l_{t+k} = l_{t+k}^{(t)}$ and $l_{t+k}^* = l_{t+k}^{*,t}$ depend on the available information $\mathcal{F}_t$ at time t, this is in our case $\mathcal{T}_t$ (generated by X_k), but in practice we would of course include any information available at time t.
- The financial risk is treated exactly in the same way as the ALM risk of the life VaPo. Therefore we will no further address this problem here.

5.2 Construction of the VaPo

Let $\mathcal{F}_t$ denote the information at time t, i.e. we assume that we have a σ-filtration $(\mathcal{F}_t)_t$ on our probability space: $\mathcal{F}_t \subset \mathcal{F}_{t+1}$.

Moreover we have assumed (Assumption 5.1) that we can decompose $(\mathcal{F}_t)$ into two independent σ-filtrations $(\mathcal{T}_t)$ and $(\mathcal{G}_t)$ such that X_t is $\mathcal{T}_t$ adapted and the price process of $Z^{(t)}$ is $\mathcal{G}_t$ adapted. I.e. X_t and the price process of $Z^{(t)}$ gives an independent decomposition (in fact we even assume that $\mathcal{T}_t$ is generated by X_k).

Then we define for $k > t$

$$E_k^{(t)} = E[X_k | \mathcal{T}_t],$$ (5.9)

$$V_k^{(t)} = \mathrm{Var}(X_k | \mathcal{T}_t).$$ (5.10)

$E_k^{(t)}, E_k^{(t+1)}, \ldots$ denotes the successive sequence of forecasts for X_k (conditional expectations). Moreover the sequence forms a martingale, which means that the sequence has uncorrelated and orthogonal increments. The so-called "best estimate" prediction of the ultimate nominal claim $C_\infty = \sum_k X_k$ at time t is given by

$$E[C_\infty | \mathcal{T}_t] = C_t + \sum_{k=t+1}^{\infty} E_k^{(t)}.$$ (5.11)

We have chosen an infinite time horizon since the settlement date of an insurance claim is random.

The "best estimate" nominal reserves at time t for the remaining liabilities after time $k \geq t+1$ (including k) are given by

$$\widetilde{R}_k^{(t)} = \sum_{l=k}^{\infty} E_l^{(t)}.$$ (5.12)

Remark.
$\widetilde{R}_k^{(t)}$ are nominal reserves (not discounted values). If we choose a constant deflator $\varphi_k \equiv 1$ for all $k \geq 0$, then we obtain in view of (2.46)

$$R_k^{(k-1)} = R\left[\mathbf{X}_{(k)} \middle| \mathcal{F}_{k-1}\right] = Q_{k-1}[\mathbf{X}_{(k)}]$$ (5.13)

$$= \sum_{l=k}^{\infty} E[X_l | \mathcal{F}_{k-1}] = \sum_{l=k}^{\infty} E_l^{(k-1)} = \widetilde{R}_k^{(k-1)},$$

and analogously for constant $\varphi_k \equiv 1$

$$\widetilde{R}_k^{(t)} = Q_t[\mathbf{X}_{(k)}] = Q\left[\mathbf{X}_{(k)} \middle| \mathcal{F}_t\right].$$ (5.14)

Hence we define the valuation portfolio at time t, $\mathrm{VaPo}_{(t)}$, as follows:

period	instrument	cashflow		units
$t+1$	$Z^{(t+1)}$	X_{t+1}	$\longrightarrow$	$l_{t+1} = l_{t+1}^{(t)} = E_{t+1}^{(t)}$
$t+2$	$Z^{(t+2)}$	X_{t+2}	$\longrightarrow$	$l_{t+2} = l_{t+2}^{(t)} = E_{t+2}^{(t)}$
$\vdots$	$\vdots$	$\vdots$		$\vdots$
$t+k$	$Z^{(t+k)}$	X_{t+k}	$\longrightarrow$	$l_{t+k} = l_{t+k}^{(t)} = E_{t+k}^{(t)}$
$\vdots$	$\vdots$	$\vdots$		$\vdots$

That is,

$$\text{VaPo}_{(t)} = \sum_{k \geq 1} l_{t+k} \cdot Z^{(t+k)}. \tag{5.15}$$

Remarks.

- So far the VaPo contains only the expected liabilities (written as a portfolio). Of course we need to protect this VaPo against technical risks $l_i \mapsto l_i^*$, which will be the main subject of the remaining chapter.
- If we valuate by nominal values (the accounting principle $\mathcal{A}$ is simply adding nominal values, which corresponds to taking the deflator $\varphi_k \equiv 1$), we simply obtain the classical undiscounted best estimate claims reserves. Hence for constructing the valuation portfolio in non-life insurance one proceeds as follows: (1) Estimate nominal best estimate claims reserves $\widetilde{R}_{t+1}^{(t)}$; (2) allocate them to different time periods and appropriate financial instruments, i.e. estimate a cash flow pattern which allocates $l_{t+k}^{(t)} = E_{t+k}^{(t)}$ to, e.g., $Z^{(t+k)}$.

5.3 VaPo protected against technical risks, pragmatic approach

Our main goal is to choose a risk measure which describes the uncertainties in l_{t+k}. This risk measure should protect against adverse developments (relative to l_{t+k}) in the claims developments.

We assume that we can consider the uncertainties in the payments independently. Hence we attach to each unit a security charge as follows (**standard deviation loading**):

period	instrument	cashflow	units
$t+1$	$Z^{(t+1)}$	$X_{t+1} \longrightarrow$	$l_{t+1}^* = E_{t+1}^{(t)} + i \cdot \beta \cdot \sqrt{V_{t+1}^{(t)}}$
$t+2$	$Z^{(t+2)}$	$X_{t+2} \longrightarrow$	$l_{t+2}^* = E_{t+2}^{(t)} + i \cdot \beta \cdot \sqrt{V_{t+2}^{(t)}}$
$\vdots$	$\vdots$	$\vdots$	$\vdots$
$t+k$	$Z^{(t+k)}$	$X_{t+k} \longrightarrow$	$l_{t+k}^* = E_{t+k}^{(t)} + i \cdot \beta \cdot \sqrt{V_{t+k}^{(t)}}$
$\vdots$	$\vdots$	$\vdots$	$\vdots$

That is,

$$\text{VaPo}_{(t)}^{prot} = \sum_{k \geq 1} l_{t+k}^* \cdot Z^{(t+k)}. \tag{5.16}$$

Remarks.

- The certainty equivalent $l^*_{t+k} = l^{*,t}_{t+k}$ also depends on the time of its evaluation, i.e. on the information $\mathcal{T}_t$ which is known.

- $\beta \cdot \sqrt{V^{(t)}_{t+k}}$ stands for the risk bearing capital (risk measure). Regulatory constraints impose that the company needs to hold a risk measure in order to run the business in accounting year $t + k$ (evaluated at time t). It measures the uncertainties of $X_{t+k} | \mathcal{T}_t$ relative to $E^{(t)}_{t+k}$, and covers adverse developments in the claims payments X_{k+t}. Observe that we have chosen a standard deviation loading, i.e. the risk measure is proportional to the standard deviation of $X_{t+k} | \mathcal{T}_t$ with proportionality factor β.

- We define this risk bearing capital $\beta \cdot \sqrt{V^{(t)}_{t+k}}$ individiually for each accounting year. One should carefully do such a choice because it should also respect the dependence structures between the different accounting periods. Below we give other definitions.

- The parameter i denotes the **cost-of-capital rate**. If we want to mobilize the risk bearing capital $\beta \cdot \sqrt{V^{(t)}_{t+k}}$ from the financial market, we need to promise a return on that risk bearing capital, which is slightly higher than the riskfree rate. Because if our business runs badly, which means that we have an adverse development in X_{t+k}, we use the risk bearing capital $\beta \cdot \sqrt{V^{(t)}_{t+k}}$ to cover this adverse development. Hence, the investor's capital is exposed to risk for which he wants to obtain a price i (of course i could also depend on the time $t + k$ or could have a different financial basis, for simplicity we choose i constant).

- This means that we face two liabilities: $E^{(t)}_{t+k}$ towards to insured/injured, and $i \cdot \beta \cdot \sqrt{V^{(t)}_{t+k}}$ towards the investor/shareholder.

- It is important to distinguish between
  - price for capital exposed to risk $i \cdot \beta \cdot \sqrt{V^{(t)}_{t+k}}$
  - availability of the capital exposed to risk $\beta \cdot \sqrt{V^{(t)}_{t+k}}$.

  Observe that we only hold the capital that is needed to recrute the risk measure (price of risk measure). It is then the task of the regulator to make sure that the insurance company really recrutes/holds that risk bearing capital. Moreover, holding the price for the risk bearing capital does not guarantee its availability when it is due. Henceforth, i has to be so large that risk measure can really be recruted at that price.

- $\beta \cdot \sqrt{V^{(t)}_{t+k}}$ can be motivated by the Swiss Solvency Test approach: risk is considered one a 1-year time horizon. As risk measure one considers expected shortfall at some level $\alpha > 0$: $\mathrm{VaR}_\alpha(X)$ is the α-quantile of X, then the expected shortfall of X at level α is given by (losses are positive)

$$\mathrm{ES}_\alpha(X) = E\left[X|\, X > \mathrm{VaR}_\alpha(X)\right]. \tag{5.17}$$

If X is normally distributed, then both, the Value-at-Risk $\mathrm{VaR}_\alpha(X)$ and the expected shortfall $\mathrm{ES}_\alpha(X)$, are multiples (β) of the standard deviation.

- In this construction we consider each accounting year, X_{t+k} respectively, individually. Pay attention to the fact that the single cash flows are not necessarily independent, which may have various impacts on simultaneous risk capital calculations for all future accounting years.

- **We conclude.** Both, the choice of the risk measure and the cost-of-capital rate, are rather ad-hoc. Many solvency systems, for example the Swiss Solvency Test [SST06], use such an ad-hoc solution. To obtain a unified approach using economic theory, financial mathematics and actuarial sciences much more research (and deeper mathematical methods) are needed. First attempts are done for example on the field of indifference pricing (see Malamud et al. [MTW07]). In most of these developments the models and methods need to be further refined so that, e.g., the role of the regulator is modelled realistically.

5.4 VaPo protected against technical risks, theoretical considerations

In this section we use utility theory to motivate a risk margin: Choose $l^*_{t+k} = l^{*(\alpha)}_{t+k}$, where $l^{*(\alpha)}_{t+k}$ is a certainty equivalent at time t for payments in period $k + t$ with risk aversion α (for the explicit definition see below). Hence the margin is given by

$$l^{*(\alpha)}_{t+k} - E^{(t)}_{t+k}. \tag{5.18}$$

We construct the certainty equivalent $l^{*(\alpha)}_{t+k}$ as follows:

Utility Theory. If we have two random variables W and V we introduce a preference ordering. Say: We prefer V over W, write $V \succeq W$.

Neumann-Morgenstern, 1944 (Theory of games and economic behaviour): Reasonable preference orderings can be understood as expected utilities. Choose a utility function $u : \mathbb{R} \to \mathbb{R}$ with $u(0) = 0$ and $u' > 0$. If we have risk aversion we need to choose u such that $u'' < 0$. Hence we define the preference ordering by

$$V \succeq W \quad \Leftrightarrow \quad E[u(V)] \geq E[u(W)]. \tag{5.19}$$

$u(x)$ indicates the utility that is located in the monetary unit x. One of the most popular utility functions is the exponential utility function: $u(x) = 1 - \exp\{-\alpha x\}$ with constant $\alpha > 0$ (see Figure 5.2).

The exponential utility function has constant risk aversion given by

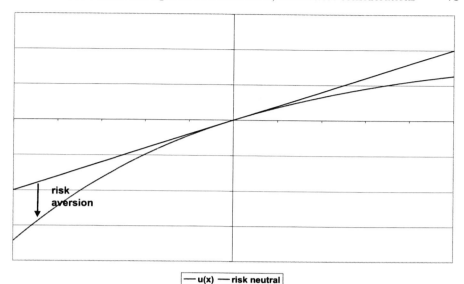

$$-u(x) \quad -\text{risk neutral}$$

Fig. 5.2. Risk aversion for utility function $u(x) = 1 - \exp\{-\alpha x\}$

$$-\frac{u''(x)}{u'(x)} = \alpha. \tag{5.20}$$

Hence the risk aversion is for the exponential utility function parametrized by α.

A second popular utility function used is the so-called power utility that is not further discussed here (see Cochrane [Co01]).

The zero utility principle from our point of view with utility function u means that we are willing to replace the random variable $X_{t+k}|\mathcal{T}_t$ by a fixed amount $l_{t+k}^{*(\alpha)}$ such that the expected utility is the same, i.e.

$$E\left[u(-X_{t+k})| \mathcal{T}_t\right] = u(-l_{t+k}^{*(\alpha)}), \tag{5.21}$$

i.e. we are willing to pay the deterministic premium $l_{t+k}^{*(\alpha)} \geq E_{t+k}^{(t)}$, since (using concavity and Jensen's inequality)

$$u(-l_{t+k}^{*(\alpha)}) \leq u\left(-E\left[X_{k+t}| \mathcal{T}_t\right]\right) = u\left(-E_{t+k}^{(t)}\right). \tag{5.22}$$

If we work with the exponential utility function then the price we are willing to pay is given by

$$E\left[u(-X_{t+k})| \mathcal{T}_t\right] = 1 - E\left[\exp\{-\alpha(-X_{t+k})\}| \mathcal{T}_t\right] \tag{5.23}$$
$$= 1 - \exp\{-\alpha(-l_{t+k}^{*(\alpha)})\}.$$

This implies that

$$l_{t+k}^{*(\alpha)} = \frac{1}{\alpha} \log E\left[\exp\{-\alpha(-X_{t+k})\}|\, \mathcal{T}_t\right] \tag{5.24}$$

$$= E_{t+k}^{(t)} + \frac{1}{\alpha} \log E\left[\exp\left\{\alpha\left(X_{t+k} - E_{t+k}^{(t)}\right)\right\}\Big|\, \mathcal{T}_t\right]$$

$$\approx E_{t+k}^{(t)} + \frac{\alpha}{2} \cdot V_{t+k}^{(t)},$$

where in the last step we have used a Taylor approximation.

Hence this gives the following VaPo protected against technical risks (**Variance loading**):

period	instrument	cashflow	units
$t+1$	$Z^{(t+1)}$	$X_{t+1} \longrightarrow$	$l_{t+1}^* = E_{t+1}^{(t)} + i \cdot \frac{\alpha}{2} \cdot V_{t+1}^{(t)}$
$t+2$	$Z^{(t+2)}$	$X_{t+2} \longrightarrow$	$l_{t+2}^* = E_{t+2}^{(t)} + i \cdot \frac{\alpha}{2} \cdot V_{t+2}^{(t)}$
$\vdots$	$\vdots$	$\vdots$	$\vdots$
$t+k$	$Z^{(t+k)}$	$X_{t+k} \longrightarrow$	$l_{t+k}^* = E_{t+k}^{(t)} + i \cdot \frac{\alpha}{2} \cdot V_{t+k}^{(t)}$
$\vdots$	$\vdots$	$\vdots$	$\vdots$

How do we quantify α? Using risk theory we can determine α from ruin probabilities. For details we refer to the literature on risk theory (see e.g. [Mi04]).

Remark. It may be disturbing that the pragmatic solution for the VaPo protected against technical risks uses a standard deviation approach whereas the theoretical considerations suggest a variance loading. This dilemma is also known in the framework of premium calculation principles. The variance loading violates the positive homogeneity property, which is often desirable in practice.

Question. How do we estimate $E_{t+k}^{(t)}$ and $V_{t+k}^{(t)}$ (at time t)? Pay especially attention to the fact, that these parameters need to be estimated. This immediately implies that the certainty equivalents l_{t+k}^* should also contain a **margin for parameter and model risk**.

Remark. The variance loading approach can also be seen as an Esscher premium approach. Esscher premium is popular in insurance. It is defined as follows: For $\lambda > 0$

$$H_\lambda(X_{t+k}|\mathcal{T}_t) = \frac{E\left[\exp\{\lambda \cdot X_{t+k}\} \cdot X_{t+k}|\, \mathcal{T}_t\right]}{E\left[\exp\{\lambda \cdot X_{t+k}\}|\, \mathcal{T}_t\right]}, \tag{5.25}$$

subject to the condition

$$E\left[\exp\{\lambda \cdot X_{t+k}\}|\,\mathcal{T}_t\right] < \infty. \tag{5.26}$$

For $\lambda \to 0$ we have

$$H_\lambda(X_{t+k}|\mathcal{T}_t) = E\left[X_{t+k}|\,\mathcal{T}_t\right] + \lambda \cdot \mathrm{Var}\left[X_{t+k}|\,\mathcal{T}_t\right] + o(\lambda). \tag{5.27}$$

For normally distributed random variables the Esscher premium is exact ($o(\lambda) = 0$). In [Wa02] and [La04] there is the Esscher premium also defined for exponential and elliptical tilting which enables to consider loadings for dependent random variables.

Pragmatic vs. theoretical approach. Observe that we have not said anything about the dependence structure between accounting years. If we choose the variance loading in each accounting year and then simply add the risk measures to obtain the overall loading, we assume that the accounting year payments are independent. On the other hand, if we add risk measures from standard deviation loadings, we are rather on the safe side, because this approach would be implied by assuming total positive correlation between accounting year payments.

5.5 Loss development triangles

5.5.1 Definitions

Pooling data and claims occurence principle:

Usually, in non-life insurance data are pooled so that one obtains homogeneous groups. For example, for pricing one builds homogeneous subportfolios which are then evaluated. For claims reserving one typically builds different subportfolios consisting of different lines of business, claims types, etc. These subportfolios are then further structured by a time component like the accident year.

There are different methodologies to set an accident year, e.g. underwriting year principle, accident date principle, claims-made principle, etc. The insurance contract rules exactly which claims within which time period are covered by the premium. In order to do a meaningful analysis it is important that the choice of the premium principle and the accident date principle are compatible, when pooling data for the study of loss development triangles.

Then claims data are typically structured in triangle form where the vertical axis structures the accident years i and the horizontal axis the development years j.

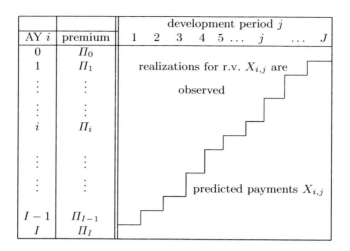

$X_{i,j}$ denotes the payments for accident year i in development period $j \geq 1$ and $X_{i,0} = -\Pi_i$ denote the premiums received for accident year i (at the beginning of accident year i). Cumulative claims payments for accident year i within the first j development periods are given by

$$C_{i,j} = \sum_{k=1}^{j} X_{i,k}. \tag{5.28}$$

If we want to have all claim payments within a fixed accounting year we should consider

$$X_k = \sum_{i+j=k} X_{i,j}, \tag{5.29}$$

these are the diagonals of our loss development rectangles.

Example 5.1 (Non-life development triangles).

For our example we use the Taylor-Ashe [TA83] data, which were also used by Verrall [Ve90], [Ve91] and Mack [Ma93] (cf. Table 1 in [Ma93]).

Incremental payments $X_{i,j}$

	1	2	3	4	5	6	7	8	9	10
0	357'848	766'940	610'542	482'940	527'326	574'398	146'342	139'950	227'229	67'948
1	352'118	884'021	933'894	1'183'289	445'745	320'996	527'804	266'172	425'046	
2	290'507	1'001'799	926'219	1'016'654	750'816	146'923	495'992	280'405		
3	310'608	1'108'250	776'189	1'562'400	272'482	352'053	206'286			
4	443'160	693'190	991'983	769'488	504'851	470'639				
5	396'132	937'085	847'498	805'037	705'960					
6	440'832	847'631	1'131'398	1'063'269						
7	359'480	1'061'648	1'443'370							
8	376'686	986'608								
9	344'014									

Cumulative payments $C_{i,j}$

	1	2	3	4	5	6	7	8	9	10
0	357'848	1'124'788	1'735'330	2'218'270	2'745'596	3'319'994	3'466'336	3'606'286	3'833'515	3'901'463
1	352'118	1'236'139	2'170'033	3'353'322	3'799'067	4'120'063	4'647'867	4'914'039	5'339'085	
2	290'507	1'292'306	2'218'525	3'235'179	3'985'995	4'132'918	4'628'910	4'909'315		
3	310'608	1'418'858	2'195'047	3'757'447	4'029'929	4'381'982	4'588'268			
4	443'160	1'136'350	2'128'333	2'897'821	3'402'672	3'873'311				
5	396'132	1'333'217	2'180'715	2'985'752	3'691'712					
6	440'832	1'288'463	2'419'861	3'483'130						
7	359'480	1'421'128	2'864'498							
8	376'686	1'363'294								
9	344'014									

Accounting year payments X_k

1	2	3	4	5	6	7	8	9	10
357'848	1'119'058	1'785'070	2'729'241	4'188'244	3'902'308	5'150'454	3'911'256	5'221'066	5'993'545

5.5.2 Chain-ladder method

Probably the most popular method to predict future claims payments is the so-called chain-ladder method. For our exposition we revisit this method since we will use it to construct the valuation portfolio. For other methods and more background information we refer to Taylor [Ta00].

Assume I is the last year for which we have received the premium. Define

$$\mathcal{B}_k = \sigma\{X_{i,j} : i + j \leq I, j \leq k\} = \sigma\{C_{i,j} : i + j \leq I, j \leq k\}. \qquad (5.30)$$

Hence $\mathcal{B}_J$ is σ-field in the upper triangle, where we have observations at time I.

Model Assumptions 5.3 (Chain-ladder model) *We assume that*

- *the filtration $\mathcal{T}_t$ is generated by $\{C_{i,j} : i + j \leq t\}$,*
- *payments $X_{i,j}$ in different accident years i are independent,*
- *$(C_{i,j})_{j\geq0}$ is a Markov chain and there exist $f_0 < 0$ and $f_j > 0$ $(j \geq 1)$ and σ_j^2 $(j \geq 0)$ such that for all $i \leq I$ and $j \geq 1$*

$$E[C_{i,j} \,|\, C_{i,j-1}] = f_{j-1} \cdot C_{i,j-1}, \qquad (5.31)$$

$$\mathrm{Var}(C_{i,j} \,|\, C_{i,j-1}) = \sigma_{j-1}^2 \cdot C_{i,j-1}. \qquad (5.32)$$

Remarks.

- There is a huge literature on the chain-ladder method. One of the first rigorous probabilistic approach to the chain-ladder method is due to Mack [Ma93]. Mack has given a distribution-free stochastic model for the chain-ladder method in which he derived an estimate for the mean square error of prediction (MSEP).
- f_j are called chain-ladder factors, development factors or age-to-age factors.
- Define the individual development factors

$$F_{i,j} = \frac{C_{i,j+1}}{C_{i,j}}, \qquad (5.33)$$

then $F_{i,j}$ are conditionally, given $\mathcal{B}_j$, unbiased estimators for f_j with conditional variance

$$\mathrm{Var}(F_{i,j} \,|\, \mathcal{B}_j) = \sigma_j^2 / C_{i,j}. \qquad (5.34)$$

The chain-ladder model immediately implies, how we should predict the ultimate claim $C_{i,\infty} = C_{i,J}$ and the incremental payments $X_{i,j}$ for $i + j > I$:

Lemma 5.2. *Under Assumptions 5.3 we have for all $i \geq 0$, $j < J$, $k \geq 1$*

$$E\left[C_{i,J} \mid C_{i,j}\right] = C_{i,j} \cdot f_j \cdots f_{J-1}, \tag{5.35}$$

$$E\left[X_{i,j+k} \mid C_{i,j}\right] = C_{i,j} \cdot f_j \cdots f_{j+k-2} \cdot \left(f_{j+k-1} - 1\right). \tag{5.36}$$

Proof. This is an exercise using conditional expectations

$$E\left[C_{i,J} \mid C_{i,j}\right] = E\left[E\left[C_{i,J} \mid C_{i,J-1}\right] \mid C_{i,j}\right]$$
$$= f_{J-1} \cdot E\left[C_{i,J-1} \mid C_{i,j}\right]. \tag{5.37}$$

If we iterate this procedure until we reach j we obtain the first result. The second assertion easily follows from $X_{i,j+k} = C_{i,j+k} - C_{i,j+k-1}$.

$\square$

From Lemma 5.2 we see that under the chain-ladder model assumptions ($\mathcal{T}_t = \mathcal{B}_J$ for $t = I$)

$$E^{(t)}_{t+k} = E\left[X_{t+k} \mid \mathcal{T}_t\right] = \sum_{i+j=t+k} E\left[X_{i,j} \mid \mathcal{B}_J\right] \tag{5.38}$$

$$= \sum_{i+j=t} C_{i,j} \cdot f_j \cdots f_{j+k-2} \cdot \left(f_{j+k-1} - 1\right),$$

hence there remains to estimate the chain-ladder factors f_j.

We introduce the following notations ($J = I = t$)

$$i^*(j) = I - j \quad \text{and} \quad j^*(i) = J - i, \tag{5.39}$$

hence $X_{i^*(j),j}$ and $X_{i,j^*(i)}$ belong to the last observed accounting year. Estimators for f_j and σ_j^2 are

$$\widehat{f}_j = \frac{\sum_{i=0}^{i^*(j+1)} C_{i,j+1}}{\sum_{i=0}^{i^*(j+1)} C_{i,j}} = \sum_{i=0}^{i^*(j+1)} \frac{C_{i,j}}{\sum_{i=0}^{i^*(j+1)} C_{i,j}} \cdot F_{i,j}, \tag{5.40}$$

$$\widehat{\sigma}_j^2 = \frac{1}{i^*(j+1)} \cdot \sum_{i=0}^{i^*(j+1)} C_{i,j} \cdot \left(\frac{C_{i,j+1}}{C_{i,j}} - \widehat{f}_j\right)^2.$$

Hence choose on the set $\mathcal{T}_t$ the following chain-ladder estimators for l_{t+k}

$$l_{t+k} = \widehat{E^{(t)}_{t+k}} = \sum_{i+j=t} C_{i,j} \cdot \widehat{f}_j \cdots \widehat{f}_{j+k-2} \cdot \left(\widehat{f}_{j+k-1} - 1\right). \tag{5.41}$$

Lemma 5.3. *Conditionally, given $\mathcal{B}_j$, $\widehat{f}_j$ are unbiased estimators for f_j.*

This immediately implies that $\widehat{f}_j$ are unbiased estimators for f_j.

Proof of Lemma 5.3.

$$E\left[\widehat{f}_j \middle| \mathcal{B}_j\right] = E\left[\frac{\sum_{i=0}^{i^*(j+1)} C_{i,j+1}}{\sum_{i=0}^{i^*(j+1)} C_{i,j}} \middle| \mathcal{B}_j\right] \tag{5.42}$$

$$= \frac{E\left[\sum_{i=0}^{i^*(j+1)} C_{i,j+1} \middle| \mathcal{B}_j\right]}{\sum_{i=0}^{i^*(j+1)} C_{i,j}} = f_j.$$

This finishes the proof of Lemma 5.3.

$\square$

Lemma 5.4. *Choose $l \leq k < j$. Then $\widehat{f}_j$ and $\widehat{f}_k$ are conditionally uncorrelated, given $\mathcal{B}_l$.*

This also immediately implies the unconditional uncorrelatedness of the estimators $\widehat{f}_j$ and $\widehat{f}_k$.

Proof of Lemma 5.4. Assume $j > k \geq l$. Then

$$E\left[\widehat{f}_j \cdot \widehat{f}_k \middle| \mathcal{B}_l\right] = E\left[\widehat{f}_k \cdot E\left[\widehat{f}_j \middle| \mathcal{B}_j\right] \middle| \mathcal{B}_l\right] = E\left[\widehat{f}_k \cdot f_j \middle| \mathcal{B}_l\right] = f_k \cdot f_j. \tag{5.43}$$

This finishes the proof of Lemma 5.4.

$\square$

An immediate consequence is the next corollary

Corollary 5.4 *Choose $j > j^*(i)$. The chain-ladder estimator given by*

$$\widehat{X}_{i,j} = C_{i,j^*(i)} \cdot \widehat{f}_{j^*(i)} \cdots \widehat{f}_{j-2} \cdot \left(\widehat{f}_{j-1} - 1\right) \tag{5.44}$$

is conditionally unbiased for $E\left[X_{i,j} \middle| \mathcal{T}_t\right]$, given $\mathcal{B}_{j^*(i)}$ or $C_{i,j^*(i)}$, respectively.

Proof. We have

$$E\left[\widehat{X}_{i,j} \middle| \mathcal{B}_{j^*(i)}\right] = C_{i,j^*(i)} \cdot E\left[\widehat{f}_{j^*(i)} \cdots \widehat{f}_{j-2} \cdot \left(\widehat{f}_{j-1} - 1\right) \middle| \mathcal{B}_{j^*(i)}\right]$$

$$= E\left[X_{i,j} \middle| \mathcal{T}_t\right], \tag{5.45}$$

where in the last step we have used the conditional unbiasedness and uncorrelatedness of the $\widehat{f}_j$, the independence of different accident years and the Markov property of our time series.

$\square$

Hence this motivates

$$\widehat{E_{t+k}^{(t)}} = \sum_{i+j=t+k} \widehat{X}_{i,j}, \tag{5.46}$$

which is exactly (5.41).

Lemma 5.5. $\widehat{f}_j$ *is the $\mathcal{B}_{j+1}$-measurable unbiased estimator, which has minimal conditional variance among all linear combinations of unbiased estimators of $F_{i,j} = C_{i,j+1}/C_{i,j}$, given $\mathcal{B}_j$.*

Proof. See Taylor [Ta00], Proposition 12.1 (the proof is based on the method of Lagrange).

$\square$

Lemma 5.6. $\widehat{\sigma}_j^2$ *are conditionally unbiased estimators for σ_j^2, given $\mathcal{B}_j$.*

Proof of Lemma 5.6. We have

$$E\left[\left(\frac{C_{i,k+1}}{C_{i,k}} - \widehat{f}_k\right)^2 \middle| \mathcal{B}_k\right] = E\left[\left(\frac{C_{i,k+1}}{C_{i,k}} - f_k\right)^2 \middle| \mathcal{B}_k\right] \tag{5.47}$$

$$-2 \cdot E\left[\left(\frac{C_{i,k+1}}{C_{i,k}} - f_k\right) \cdot \left(\widehat{f}_k - f_k\right) \middle| \mathcal{B}_k\right] + E\left[\left(\widehat{f}_k - f_k\right)^2 \middle| \mathcal{B}_k\right].$$

Hence we calculate the terms on the r.h.s. of the equality above.

$$E\left[\left(\frac{C_{i,k+1}}{C_{i,k}} - f_k\right)^2 \middle| \mathcal{B}_k\right] = \mathrm{Var}\left(\frac{C_{i,k+1}}{C_{i,k}} \middle| \mathcal{B}_k\right) = \frac{1}{C_{i,k}} \cdot \sigma_k^2. \tag{5.48}$$

The next term is (using the independence of different accident years)

$$E\left[\left(\frac{C_{i,k+1}}{C_{i,k}} - f_k\right) \cdot \left(\widehat{f}_k - f_k\right) \middle| \mathcal{B}_k\right] = \mathrm{Cov}\left(\frac{C_{i,k+1}}{C_{i,k}}, \widehat{f}_k \middle| \mathcal{B}_k\right) \tag{5.49}$$

$$= \frac{C_{i,k}}{\sum_i C_{i,k}} \cdot \mathrm{Var}\left(\frac{C_{i,k+1}}{C_{i,k}} \middle| \mathcal{B}_k\right)$$

$$= \frac{\sigma_k^2}{\sum_i C_{i,k}}.$$

Whereas for the last term we obtain

$$E\left[\left(\widehat{f}_k - f_k\right)^2 \middle| \mathcal{B}_k\right] = \mathrm{Var}\left(\widehat{f}_k \middle| \mathcal{B}_k\right) = \frac{\sigma_k^2}{\sum_i C_{i,k}}. \tag{5.50}$$

Putting all this together gives

$$E\left[\left(\frac{C_{i,k+1}}{C_{i,k}} - \widehat{f}_k\right)^2 \middle| \mathcal{B}_k\right] = \sigma_k^2 \cdot \left(\frac{1}{C_{i,k}} - \frac{1}{\sum_i C_{i,k}}\right). \tag{5.51}$$

Hence we have

$$E\left[\widehat{\sigma}_k^2 \middle| \mathcal{B}_k\right] = \frac{1}{i^*(k+1)} \cdot \sum_{i=0}^{i^*(k+1)} C_{i,k} \cdot E\left[\left(\frac{C_{i,k+1}}{C_{i,k}} - \widehat{f}_k\right)^2 \middle| \mathcal{B}_k\right] = \sigma_k^2, \tag{5.52}$$

which proves the claim of Lemma 5.6.

□

We will also need the following equality

$$E\left[\widehat{f}_k^2 \middle| \mathcal{B}_k\right] = \operatorname{Var}\left(\widehat{f}_k \middle| \mathcal{B}_k\right) + f_k^2 = \frac{\sigma_k^2}{\sum_{i=0}^{i^*(k+1)} C_{i,k}} + f_k^2. \tag{5.53}$$

Example 5.1 (revisited).

Observed individual chain-ladder factors $F_{i,j}$.

	1	2	3	4	5	6	7	8	9
0	3.1432	1.5428	1.2783	1.2377	1.2092	1.0441	1.0404	1.0630	1.0177
1	3.5106	1.7555	1.5453	1.1329	1.0845	1.1281	1.0573	1.0865	
2	4.4485	1.7167	1.4583	1.2321	1.0369	1.1200	1.0606		
3	4.5680	1.5471	1.7118	1.0725	1.0874	1.0471			
4	2.5642	1.8730	1.3615	1.1742	1.1383				
5	3.3656	1.6357	1.3692	1.2364					
6	2.9228	1.8781	1.4394						
7	3.9533	2.0157							
8	3.6192								
9									
$\widehat{f}_j$	3.4906	1.7473	1.4574	1.1739	1.1038	1.0863	1.0539	1.0766	1.0177
$\widehat{\sigma}_j$	400.35	194.26	204.85	123.22	117.18	90.48	21.13	33.87	21.13

Note that we do not have enough data to estimate the last variance parameter σ_9^2. Therefore to estimate σ_9^2 we have chosen the formula given in [Ma93] ($J = 10$):

$$\widehat{\sigma_{J-1}^2} = \min\left\{\widehat{\sigma}_{J-2}^4 / \widehat{\sigma}_{J-3}^2; \widehat{\sigma}_{J-2}^2; \widehat{\sigma}_{J-3}^2\right\}. \tag{5.54}$$

This gives the following completed (estimated) claims development triangle for the cumulative payments $C_{i,j}$:

Predicted cumulative payments $C_{i,j}$

	1	2	3	4	5	6	7	8	9	10
0	357'848	1'124'788	1'735'330	2'218'270	2'745'596	3'319'994	3'466'336	3'606'286	3'833'515	3'901'463
1	352'118	1'236'139	2'170'033	3'353'322	3'799'067	4'120'063	4'647'867	4'914'039	5'339'085	5'433'719
2	290'507	1'292'306	2'218'525	3'235'179	3'985'995	4'132'918	4'628'910	4'909'315	5'285'148	5'378'826
3	310'608	1'418'858	2'195'047	3'757'447	4'029'929	4'381'982	4'588'268	4'835'458	5'205'637	5'297'906
4	443'160	1'136'350	2'128'333	2'897'821	3'402'672	3'873'311	4'207'459	4'434'133	4'773'589	4'858'200
5	396'132	1'333'217	2'180'715	2'985'752	3'691'712	4'074'999	4'426'546	4'665'023	5'022'155	5'111'171
6	440'832	1'288'463	2'419'861	3'483'130	4'088'678	4'513'179	4'902'528	5'166'649	5'562'182	5'660'771
7	359'480	1'421'128	2'864'498	4'174'756	4'900'545	5'409'337	5'875'997	6'192'562	6'666'635	6'784'799
8	376'686	1'363'294	2'382'128	3'471'744	4'075'313	4'498'426	4'886'502	5'149'760	5'544'000	5'642'266
9	344'014	1'200'818	2'098'228	3'057'984	3'589'620	3'962'307	4'304'132	4'536'015	4'883'270	4'969'825

Hence the estimated expected incremental payments $(j > I - i)$

$$\widehat{E}\left[X_{i,j}\mid \mathcal{B}_J\right] = C_{i,j^*(i)} \cdot \widehat{f}_{j^*(i)} \cdots \widehat{f}_{j-2} \cdot \left(\widehat{f}_{j-1} - 1\right) \qquad (5.55)$$

are given by (see also (5.41)):

	1	2	3	4	5	6	7	8	9	10
0										
1										94'634
2									375'833	93'678
3								247'190	370'179	92'268
4							334'148	226'674	339'456	84'611
5						383'287	351'548	238'477	357'132	89'016
6					605'548	424'501	389'349	264'121	395'534	98'588
7				1'310'258	725'788	508'792	466'660	316'566	474'073	118'164
8			1'018'834	1'089'616	603'569	423'113	388'076	263'257	394'241	98'266
9		856'804	897'410	959'756	531'636	372'687	341'826	231'882	347'255	86'555

This leads to the following estimated expected payments $l_{t+k} = \widehat{E^{(t)}_{t+k}}$ in the accounting years:

$t+k$	$t+1$	$t+2$	$t+3$	$t+4$	$t+5$	$t+6$	$t+7$	$t+8$	$t+9$
l_{t+k}	5'226'536	4'179'394	3'131'668	2'127'272	1'561'879	1'177'744	744'287	445'521	86'555

Table 5.1. Estimated incremental payments

Hence we have estimated the valuation portfolio

$$\mathrm{VaPo}_{(t)} = \sum_{k\geq 1} l_{t+k} \cdot Z^{(t+k)}. \qquad (5.56)$$

If we want to obtain the cash value, we need to apply an accounting principle $\mathcal{A}$ to our valuation portfolio. We choose three different examples: 1) nominal value, 2) constant interest rate $r = 1.5\%$, 3) risk free rates used in the Swiss Solvency Field-Test 2005 (SST):

maturity	1	2	3	4	5	6	7	8	9
risk free rate	0.88%	1.14%	1.36%	1.57%	1.75%	1.91%	2.05%	2.18%	2.29%

Table 5.2. Swiss Solvency Test risk free rates 2005

This gives the following values for $\mathcal{A}_t\left(\mathrm{VaPo}_{(t)}\right)$ at time $t = J$:

	reserves $\mathcal{A}_t\left(\mathrm{VaPo}_{(t)}\right)$	difference to $\widetilde{R}^{(t)}_{t+1}$	
1) $\widehat{R}^{(t)}_{t+1}$ nominal	18'680'856		
2) $r = 1.50\%$	17'873'967	806'888	4.32%
3) SST rates	17'847'512	833'344	4.46%

Table 5.3. Monetary value of the valuation portfolio for different accounting principles

$\square$

5.5.3 Estimation of the technical risks in the chain-ladder model, single accident year

Let us, for the moment, fix one single accident year i. Hence, under the chain-ladder Assumptions 5.3 we have for $t = I$, $k \geq 1$

$$E_{t+k}^{(t)}(i) = E\left[X_{i,j^*(i)+k}\big|\mathcal{T}_t\right] = E\left[X_{i,j^*(i)+k}\big|C_{i,j^*(i)}\right], \qquad (5.57)$$

which is estimated by (see also (5.55))

$$l_{t+k}(i) = \widehat{E_{t+k}^{(t)}}(i) = C_{i,j^*(i)} \cdot \prod_{l=0}^{k-2} \widehat{f}_{j^*(i)+l} \cdot \left(\widehat{f}_{j^*(i)+k-1} - 1\right). \qquad (5.58)$$

This gives the following VaPo for accident year i:

period	instrument	cashflow	units
$t+1$	$Z^{(t+1)}$	X_{t+1}	$\rightarrow l_{t+1}(i) = C_{i,j^*(i)} \cdot \left(\widehat{f}_{j^*(i)} - 1\right)$
$t+2$	$Z^{(t+2)}$	X_{t+2}	$\rightarrow l_{t+2}(i) = C_{i,j^*(i)} \cdot \widehat{f}_{j^*(i)} \cdot \left(\widehat{f}_{j^*(i)+1} - 1\right)$
$\vdots$	$\vdots$	$\vdots$	$\vdots$
$t+k$	$Z^{(t+k)}$	X_{t+k}	$\rightarrow l_{t+k}(i) = C_{i,j^*(i)} \prod_{l=0}^{k-2} \widehat{f}_{j^*(i)+l} \left(\widehat{f}_{j^*(i)+k-1} - 1\right)$
$\vdots$	$\vdots$	$\vdots$	

That is,

$$\text{VaPo}_{(t)}(i) = \sum_{k \geq 1} l_{t+k}(i) \cdot Z^{(t+k)}. \qquad (5.59)$$

First approach to the technical risk

As in (5.10) we set for accident year i

$$V_{t+k}^{(t)}(i) = \text{Var}\left(X_{i,j^*(i)+k}\big|\mathcal{T}_t\right) = \text{Var}\left(X_{i,j^*(i)+k}\big|C_{i,j^*(i)}\right), \qquad (5.60)$$

$$W_{t+k}^{(t)}(i) = \text{Var}\left(C_{i,j^*(i)+k}\big|C_{i,j^*(i)}\right). \qquad (5.61)$$

If we decompose the variance in its usual way we obtain

$$W_{t+k}^{(t)}(i) = E\left[\text{Var}\left(C_{i,j^*(i)+k}\big|C_{i,j^*(i)+k-1}\right)\big|C_{i,j^*(i)}\right] \qquad (5.62)$$
$$+ \text{Var}\left(E\left[C_{i,j^*(i)+k}\big|C_{i,j^*(i)+k-1}\right]\big|C_{i,j^*(i)}\right)$$
$$= E\left[\sigma_{j^*(i)+k-1}^2 \cdot C_{i,j^*(i)+k-1}\big|C_{i,j^*(i)}\right]$$
$$+ \text{Var}\left(f_{j^*(i)+k-1} \cdot C_{i,j^*(i)+k-1}\big|C_{i,j^*(i)}\right)$$
$$= \sigma_{j^*(i)+k-1}^2 \cdot C_{i,j^*(i)} \cdot \prod_{l=j^*(i)}^{j^*(i)+k-2} f_l$$
$$+ f_{j^*(i)+k-1}^2 \cdot \text{Var}\left(C_{i,j^*(i)+k-1}\big|C_{i,j^*(i)}\right)$$
$$= \sigma_{j^*(i)+k-1}^2 \cdot C_{i,j^*(i)} \cdot \prod_{l=j^*(i)}^{j^*(i)+k-2} f_l + f_{j^*(i)+k-1}^2 \cdot W_{t+k-1}^{(t)}(i).$$

Remark: The first term on the r.h.s. of the equality above can be rewritten with

$$E\left[C_{i,j^*(i)+k-1}\,\middle|\,C_{i,j^*(i)}\right] = C_{i,j^*(i)} \cdot \prod_{l=j^*(i)}^{j^*(i)+k-2} f_l. \tag{5.63}$$

Hence we have found an iteration for the conditional variances, which immediately implies

$$W_{t+k}^{(t)}(i) = C_{i,j^*(i)} \cdot \sum_{m=j^*(i)}^{j^*(i)+k-1} \prod_{n=m+1}^{j^*(i)+k-1} f_n^2 \cdot \sigma_m^2 \cdot \prod_{l=j^*(i)}^{m-1} f_l \tag{5.64}$$

$$= \sum_{m=j^*(i)}^{j^*(i)+k-1} \prod_{n=m+1}^{j^*(i)+k-1} f_n^2 \cdot \sigma_m^2 \cdot E\left[C_{i,m}\,\middle|\,C_{i,j^*(i)}\right].$$

If we insert the estimators for f_l and σ_l^2 (estimated from $\mathcal{B}_J$) we obtain an estimator for the conditional variances of the cumulative payments.

$$\widehat{W_{t+k}^{(t)}}(i) = C_{i,j^*(i)} \cdot \sum_{m=j^*(i)}^{j^*(i)+k-1} \prod_{n=m+1}^{j^*(i)+k-1} \widehat{f}_n^2 \cdot \widehat{\sigma}_m^2 \cdot \prod_{l=j^*(i)}^{m-1} \widehat{f}_l \tag{5.65}$$

$$= \sum_{m=j^*(i)}^{j^*(i)+k-1} \prod_{n=m+1}^{j^*(i)+k-1} \widehat{f}_n^2 \cdot \widehat{\sigma}_m^2 \cdot \widehat{C}_{i,m}$$

$$= \widehat{C}_{i,j^*(i)+k}^2 \sum_{m=j^*(i)}^{j^*(i)+k-1} \frac{\widehat{\sigma}_m^2 / \widehat{f}_m^2}{\widehat{C}_{i,m}},$$

with

$$\widehat{C}_{i,m} = \widehat{E}\left[C_{i,m}\,\middle|\,C_{i,j^*(i)}\right] = C_{i,j^*(i)} \cdot \prod_{l=j^*(i)}^{m-1} \widehat{f}_l. \tag{5.66}$$

For the incremental payments we have

$$V_{t+k}^{(t)}(i) = E\left[\mathrm{Var}\left(X_{i,j^*(i)+k}\,\middle|\,C_{i,j^*(i)+k-1}\right)\middle|\,C_{i,j^*(i)}\right]$$

$$+ \mathrm{Var}\left(E\left[X_{i,j^*(i)+k}\,\middle|\,C_{i,j^*(i)+k-1}\right]\middle|\,C_{i,j^*(i)}\right)$$

$$= E\left[\sigma_{j^*(i)+k-1}^2 \cdot C_{i,j^*(i)+k-1}\,\middle|\,C_{i,j^*(i)}\right]$$

$$+ \mathrm{Var}\left(\left(f_{j^*(i)+k-1} - 1\right) \cdot C_{i,j^*(i)+k-1}\,\middle|\,C_{i,j^*(i)}\right). \tag{5.67}$$

Hence we obtain the following estimator for the variance:

Estimator 5.5 (Process variance for single accident years)

$$\widehat{V_{t+k}^{(t)}}(i) = \widehat{\sigma}_{j^*(i)+k-1}^2 \cdot C_{i,j^*(i)} \cdot \prod_{l=j^*(i)}^{j^*(i)+k-2} \widehat{f_l} + \left(\widehat{f}_{j^*(i)+k-1} - 1\right)^2 \cdot \widehat{W_{t+k-1}^{(t)}}(i)$$

$$= \widehat{C}_{i,j^*(i)+k}^2 \cdot \frac{\widehat{\sigma}_{j^*(i)+k-1}^2 / \widehat{f}_{j^*(i)+k-1}^2}{\widehat{C}_{i,j^*(i)+k-1}} + \left(\widehat{f}_{j^*(i)+k-1} - 1\right)^2 \cdot \widehat{W_{t+k-1}^{(t)}}(i)$$

$$= \widehat{W_{t+k}^{(t)}}(i) + \left(1 - 2 \cdot \widehat{f}_{j^*(i)+k-1}\right) \cdot \widehat{W_{t+k-1}^{(t)}}(i). \qquad (5.68)$$

Using the pragmatic approach (first approach with standard deviation loadings), we obtain for the VaPo protected against technical risks (see (5.58) and (5.68)) for a single accident year i:

period	instrument	cashflow	units
$t+1$	$Z^{(t+1)}$	$X_{t+1} \longrightarrow l_{t+1}^*(i) = \widehat{E_{t+1}^{(t)}}(i) + i \cdot \beta \cdot \widehat{V_{t+1}^{(t)}}(i)^{1/2}$	
$t+2$	$Z^{(t+2)}$	$X_{t+2} \longrightarrow l_{t+2}^*(i) = \widehat{E_{t+2}^{(t)}}(i) + i \cdot \beta \cdot \widehat{V_{t+2}^{(t)}}(i)^{1/2}$	
$\vdots$	$\vdots$	$\vdots$	$\vdots$
$t+k$	$Z^{(t+k)}$	$X_{t+k} \longrightarrow l_{t+k}^*(i) = \widehat{E_{t+k}^{(t)}}(i) + i \cdot \beta \cdot \widehat{V_{t+k}^{(t)}}(i)^{1/2}$	
$\vdots$	$\vdots$	$\vdots$	$\vdots$

That is,

$$\text{VaPo}_{(t)}^{prot}(i) = \sum_{k \geq 1} l_{t+k}^*(i) \cdot Z^{(t+k)}. \qquad (5.69)$$

Example 5.1 (revisited).

We calculate the uncertainties $\widehat{V_{t+k}^{(t)}}(i)^{1/2}$ which correspond to estimated incremental payments $X_{i,j^*(i)+k}$ on page 82 (see also (5.55)).

	1	2	3	4	5	6	7	8	9	10
0										
1										48'832
2									75'052	48'603
3								45'268	74'566	48'243
4							178'062	44'398	72'835	46'336
5						225'149	183'669	47'407	77'269	47'781
6					229'965	238'145	194'528	52'055	84'306	50'590
7				346'712	258'879	264'121	216'465	62'761	100'344	56'248
8			226'818	332'762	242'972	244'204	200'828	62'482	98'906	52'140
9		234'816	275'881	364'358	250'614	240'498	199'983	74'127	115'011	51'779

The variational coefficients

$$\widehat{\mathrm{Vco}}(X_{i,j^*(i)+k}|\mathcal{B}_J) = \frac{\widehat{V_{t+k}^{(t)}}(i)^{1/2}}{\widehat{E}\left[X_{i,j^*(i)+k}|\mathcal{B}_J\right]} \tag{5.70}$$

are given by:

	1	2	3	4	5	6	7	8	9	10
0										
1										51.6%
2									20.0%	51.9%
3								18.3%	20.1%	52.3%
4							53.3%	19.6%	21.5%	54.8%
5						58.7%	52.2%	19.9%	21.6%	53.7%
6					38.0%	56.1%	50.0%	19.7%	21.3%	51.3%
7				26.5%	35.7%	51.9%	46.4%	19.8%	21.2%	47.6%
8			22.3%	30.5%	40.3%	57.7%	51.7%	23.7%	25.1%	53.1%
9		27.4%	30.7%	38.0%	47.1%	64.5%	58.5%	32.0%	33.1%	59.8%

Since we have assumed that different accident years are independent, we can simply add the second moments to obtain the estimated variance of one accounting year (pay attention to the fact, that the accounting years are not independent). Hence the overall variance of one accounting year is estimated by

$$\widehat{V_{t+k}^{(t)}} = \widehat{\mathrm{Var}}\left(X_{t+k}|\mathcal{T}_t\right) = \sum_i \widehat{\mathrm{Var}}\left(X_{i,j^*(i)+k}\big|C_{i,j^*(i)}\right) = \sum_i \widehat{V_{t+k}^{(t)}}(i). \tag{5.71}$$

Hence the estimated standard deviations for accounting years $\widehat{V_{t+k}^{(t)}}^{1/2}$ and its estimated variatonal coefficients are given by

$t+k$	$t+1$	$t+2$	$t+3$	$t+4$	$t+5$	$t+6$	$t+7$	$t+8$	$t+9$
l_{t+k}	5'226'536	4'179'394	3'131'668	2'127'272	1'561'879	1'177'744	744'287	445'521	86'555
$\widehat{V_{t+k}^{(t)}}^{1/2}$	610'035	595'147	556'123	424'414	333'918	237'751	135'798	126'278	51'779
Vco	11.7%	14.2%	17.8%	20.0%	21.4%	20.2%	18.2%	28.3%	59.8%

We define the cost-of-capital charge as follows

$$\mathrm{CoC}(k) = i \cdot \beta \cdot \widehat{V_{t+k}^{(t)}}^{1/2} \tag{5.72}$$

and the valuation portolio protected against technical risks as

$$l_{t+k}^* = l_{t+k} + \mathrm{CoC}(k), \tag{5.73}$$

with $i = 8\%$ and $\beta = \Phi^{-1}(99\%)$. Observe that in (5.73) we consider the estimated expected claims payments l_{t+k} (this is only an estimate based on

$\mathcal{B}_J$) and the cost-of-capital charge $\text{CoC}(k)$ for the valuation portfolio protected against technical risks. We do not require the availability of the capital. That is, we obtain the valuation portfolio protected against technical risks

$$\text{VaPo}_{(t)}^{prot} = \sum_{k \geq 1} l_{t+k}^* \cdot Z^{(t+k)}. \tag{5.74}$$

We obtain Table 5.4.

$t+k$	$t+1$	$t+2$	$t+3$	$t+4$	$t+5$	$t+6$	$t+7$	$t+8$	$t+9$
CoC	113'532	110'761	103'499	78'987	62'145	44'247	25'273	23'501	9'636
l_{t+k}^*	5'340'068	4'290'156	3'235'166	2'206'259	1'624'024	1'221'991	769'560	469'023	96'191

Table 5.4. Valuation portfolio protected against technical risk (process error)

Hence for the three different accounting principles (nominal, constant interest rate, risk free rates SST (see Table 5.2) we obtain Table 5.5. Table 5.5 should be compared to Table 5.3.

	VaPo	VaPo^{prot}	difference
1) nominal	18'680'856	19'252'438	571'582
2) $r = 1.50\%$	17'873'967	18'416'946	542'979
3) SST rates	17'847'512	18'387'990	540'479

Table 5.5. Monetary value of the valuation portfolio protected against technical risks (process error) for different accounting principles

$\square$

Question. As a regulator: are we satisfied with this solution? **NO!**

In fact, we have replaced the expected certainty equivalent $E_{t+k}^{(t)} + i \cdot \beta \cdot V_{t+k}^{(t)\,1/2}$ by an estimate $\widehat{E_{t+k}^{(t)}} + i \cdot \beta \cdot \widehat{V_{t+k}^{(t)}}^{\,1/2}$. This estimate covers the expected liabilities and gives a loading for the process variance. But it does not give a loading for the uncertainties in the parameter estimates (that is we have replaced the chain-ladder factors f_k by the estimators $\widehat{f}_k$).

Second approach for protection against technical risks

We consider the (conditional) **mean square error of prediction** (MSEP) which is defined as follows

$$E\left[\left(X_{i,j^*(i)+k} - \widehat{E_{t+k}^{(t)}}(i)\right)^2 \Big| \mathcal{T}_t\right]$$

$$= \text{Var}\left(X_{i,j^*(i)+k} \big| \mathcal{T}_t\right) + \left(E_{t+k}^{(t)}(i) - \widehat{E_{t+k}^{(t)}}(i)\right)^2$$

$$= V_{t+k}^{(t)}(i) + \left(E_{t+k}^{(t)}(i) - \widehat{E_{t+k}^{(t)}}(i)\right)^2, \tag{5.75}$$

note that we use that $\widehat{E_{t+k}^{(t)}}(i)$ is $\mathcal{T}_t$-measurable.

So far we have only given an estimate for the **process errors** $W_{t+k}^{(t)}(i)$ and $V_{t+k}^{(t)}(i)$ of the technical risks. Since we do not know the true parameters f_k and σ_k^2, we need to estimate them from the observations $\mathcal{T}_t$. Of course in doing so, we have an additional potential error term, the so-called **parameter error**. The parameter error is reflected by the term

$$\left(E_{t+k}^{(t)}(i) - \widehat{E_{t+k}^{(t)}}(i) \right)^2. \tag{5.76}$$

To calculate the parameter error we would have to evaluate (5.76), but this requires that the true chain-ladder factors f_k are known (which, unfortunately, is not the case). Hence in the sequel we provide an estimate for (5.76). This estimator is based on an analysis on how much the estimators $\widehat{f}_k$ fluctuate around f_k.

To get an understanding for the parameter error we introduce a time series version of the chain-ladder model (see [Mu94], [BBMW05] and [BBMW06a]).

Model Assumptions 5.6 *In addition to Model Assumptions 5.3 we assume that*

$$C_{i,j} = f_{j-1} \cdot C_{i,j-1} + \sigma_{j-1} \cdot \sqrt{C_{i,j-1}} \cdot \varepsilon_{i,j}, \tag{5.77}$$

with $\varepsilon_{i,j}$ independent, centered random variables with variance 1.

Remarks.

- We should also make sure that the $C_{i,j}$ stay positive $\mathcal{B}_0$-a.s. For the moment, we assume that this is a purely mathematical problem which is not further treated here (see also [BBMW06a]).
- (5.77) does not contradict the chain-ladder Assumptions 5.3.
- (5.77) defines an explicit stochastic model, which tells us what values our observations $\mathcal{B}_J$ could also have. In order to determine the parameter error, we need to see, how much fluctuates $\widehat{E_{t+k}^{(t)}}(i)$ around its $E_{t+k}^{(t)}(i)$ for other realizations, i.e. how would $\widehat{E_{t+k}^{(t)}}(i)$ look like, if we would have different observations?

The chain-ladder factors are (with (5.77))

$$\widehat{f}_j = \frac{\sum_{i=0}^{i^*(j+1)} C_{i,j+1}}{\sum_{i=0}^{i^*(j+1)} C_{i,j}} = f_j + \frac{\sigma_j}{\sum_{i=0}^{i^*(j+1)} C_{i,j}} \sum_{i=0}^{i^*(j+1)} (C_{i,j})^{1/2} \cdot \varepsilon_{i,j+1}. \tag{5.78}$$

There are various different ways to resample the chain-ladder factors in this time series model, and there is an extended discussion in the literature about appropriate resampling (see [BBMW06a], [MQB06] and [Gi06]). We will not further discuss this issue here: Our goal here is to conditionally resample these chain-ladder factors $\widehat{f}_j$ (this corresponds to Approach 3 in [BBMW06a]), i.e. given the observation $\mathcal{B}_j$ we resample $\widehat{f}_j$ (this is the next step in the time series). This way we obtain resampled values $\widehat{f}_j^{\mathcal{B}_j}$ by

$$\widehat{f}_j^{\mathcal{B}_j} = f_j + \frac{\sigma_j}{\sum_{i=0}^{i^*(j+1)} C_{i,j}} \sum_{i=0}^{i^*(j+1)} (C_{i,j})^{1/2} \cdot \widetilde{\varepsilon}_{i,j+1}, \qquad (5.79)$$

where $(\widetilde{\varepsilon}_{i,j})_{i,j}$ and $(\varepsilon_{i,j})_{i,j}$ are independent copies. Hence, we see that

$$\widehat{f}_j^{\mathcal{B}_j} \stackrel{(d)}{=} \widehat{f}_j \qquad \text{given } \mathcal{B}_j. \qquad (5.80)$$

If we continue this procedure in an iterative way for every j we obtain a set of random variables $\widehat{f}_0^{\mathcal{B}_0}, \ldots, \widehat{f}_{J-1}^{\mathcal{B}_{J-1}}$ which are conditionally, given $\mathcal{B}_J$, independent. $\mathcal{B}_J$ plays the role of the (deterministic) volume measure in $\widehat{f}_j$ (denominator) and we only resample the numerator of $\widehat{f}_j$ which leads to $\widehat{f}_j^{\mathcal{B}_j}$ (next step in time series).

Observe that we do not claim that $\widehat{f}_j$ are independent (in fact their squares are correlated), but we use that the conditionally resampled values are independent given $\mathcal{B}_J$ (which gives a multiplicative structure).

For simplicity, we denoted this conditional resampling measure by $P_{\mathcal{B}_J}$ and we drop the superscript $\mathcal{B}_j$ in the conditionally resampled observations $\widehat{f}_j^{\mathcal{B}_j}$. We have the following properties:

1) $\widehat{f}_1, \widehat{f}_2, \ldots$ are independent under the measure $P_{\mathcal{B}_J}$, $\qquad (5.81)$

2) $E_{\mathcal{B}_J}\left[\widehat{f}_j\right] = f_j,$ $\qquad (5.82)$

3) $\mathrm{Var}_{P_{\mathcal{B}_J}}\left(\widehat{f}_j\right) = E_{\mathcal{B}_J}\left[\widehat{f}_j^2\right] - f_j^2 = \dfrac{\sigma_j^2}{\sum_{i=0}^{i^*(j+1)} C_{i,j}}.$ $\qquad (5.83)$

Remarks.

- In fact we do not need (5.77), all that we need for the derivation of the parameter error is (5.78).
- (5.78) describes a possible model for the claims development factors. The fluctuation around f_j will be the crucial term do determine the quality of our estimate $\widehat{E_{t+k}^{(t)}}(i)$.
- In the sequel, we assume that $\mathcal{T}_t = \{C_{i,j};\ i+j \leq t\}$ is known and that we work with the conditionally resampled chain-ladder factor estimates as described above.

In the conditional resampling approach (presented in [BBMW06a]) the estimation error (5.76) for a single accident year i is estimated by

$$E_{\mathcal{B}_J}\left[\left(E_{t+k}^{(t)}(i) - \widehat{E_{t+k}^{(t)}(i)}\right)^2\right] \tag{5.84}$$

$$= C_{i,j^*(i)}^2 \cdot E_{\mathcal{B}_J}\left[\left(\prod_{l=0}^{k-2} f_{j^*(i)+l} \cdot \left(f_{j^*(i)+k-1} - 1\right)\right.\right.$$

$$\left.\left. - \prod_{l=0}^{k-2} \widehat{f}_{j^*(i)+l} \cdot \left(\widehat{f}_{j^*(i)+k-1} - 1\right)\right)^2\right].$$

Hence we need to study this last term. Due to the independence and the unbiasedness of the conditionally resampled $\widehat{f}_j$, given $\mathcal{B}_J$, we have

$$E_{\mathcal{B}_J}\left[\left(\prod_{l=0}^{k-2} f_{j^*(i)+l} \cdot \left(f_{j^*(i)+k-1} - 1\right) - \prod_{l=0}^{k-2} \widehat{f}_{j^*(i)+l} \cdot \left(\widehat{f}_{j^*(i)+k-1} - 1\right)\right)^2\right]$$

$$= \mathrm{Var}_{P_{\mathcal{B}_J}}\left(\prod_{l=0}^{k-2} \widehat{f}_{j^*(i)+l} \cdot \left(\widehat{f}_{j^*(i)+k-1} - 1\right)\right) \tag{5.85}$$

$$= E_{\mathcal{B}_J}\left[\prod_{l=0}^{k-2} \widehat{f}_{j^*(i)+l}^2 \cdot \left(\widehat{f}_{j^*(i)+k-1} - 1\right)^2\right] - \prod_{l=0}^{k-2} f_{j^*(i)+l}^2 \cdot \left(f_{j^*(i)+k-1} - 1\right)^2$$

$$= \prod_{l=0}^{k-2}\left(\frac{\sigma_{j^*(i)+l}^2}{\sum_n C_{n,j^*(i)+l}} + f_{j^*(i)+l}^2\right) \cdot \left(\frac{\sigma_{j^*(i)+k-1}^2}{\sum_n C_{n,j^*(i)+k-1}} + \left(f_{j^*(i)+k-1} - 1\right)^2\right)$$

$$- \prod_{l=0}^{k-2} f_{j^*(i)+l}^2 \cdot \left(f_{j^*(i)+k-1} - 1\right)^2.$$

This last expression can be rewritten and approximated by

$$\prod_{l=0}^{k-2} f_{j^*(i)+l}^2 \cdot \left(f_{j^*(i)+k-1} - 1\right)^2 \tag{5.86}$$

$$\cdot \left(\prod_{l=0}^{k-2}\left(\frac{\sigma_{j^*(i)+l}^2/f_{j^*(i)+l}^2}{\sum_n C_{n,j^*(i)+l}} + 1\right) \cdot \left(\frac{\sigma_{j^*(i)+k-1}^2/\left(f_{j^*(i)+k-1} - 1\right)^2}{\sum_n C_{n,j^*(i)+k-1}} + 1\right) - 1\right)$$

$$\approx \prod_{l=0}^{k-2} f_{j^*(i)+l}^2 \cdot \left(f_{j^*(i)+k-1} - 1\right)^2$$

$$\cdot \left(\sum_{l=0}^{k-2} \frac{\sigma_{j^*(i)+l}^2/f_{j^*(i)+l}^2}{\sum_n C_{n,j^*(i)+l}} + \frac{\sigma_{j^*(i)+k-1}^2/\left(f_{j^*(i)+k-1} - 1\right)^2}{\sum_n C_{n,j^*(i)+k-1}}\right).$$

In the last step we have made a linear approximation, which leads to the well-known Mack formulas [Ma93]. Henceforth the parameter error for a single accident year i is estimated by

$$\widetilde{V_{t+k}^{(t)}}(i) \stackrel{def.}{=} \widehat{E}\left[\left(E_{t+k}^{(t)}(i) - \widehat{E_{t+k}^{(t)}}(i)\right)^2 \middle| \mathcal{B}_J\right] \tag{5.87}$$

$$= \widehat{E_{t+k}^{(t)}}^2(i) \cdot \left(\sum_{l=0}^{k-2} \frac{\widehat{\sigma}_{j^*(i)+l}^2 / \widehat{f}_{j^*(i)+l}^2}{\sum_n C_{n,j^*(i)+l}} + \frac{\widehat{\sigma}_{j^*(i)+k-1}^2 / \left(\widehat{f}_{j^*(i)+k-1} - 1\right)^2}{\sum_n C_{n,j^*(i)+k-1}}\right).$$

This gives the following estimator for the conditional mean square error of prediction:

Estimator 5.7 (Conditional MSEP)

$$\widehat{E}\left[\left(X_{i,j^*(i)+k} - \widehat{E_{t+k}^{(t)}}(i)\right)^2 \middle| \mathcal{T}_t\right] = \widehat{V_{t+k}^{(t)}}(i) + \widetilde{V_{t+k}^{(t)}}(i), \tag{5.88}$$

where $\widehat{V_{t+k}^{(t)}}(i)$ is given in (5.68) and $\widetilde{V_{t+k}^{(t)}}(i)$ is given in (5.87).

Henceforth in the pragmatic approach (first version with standard devation loadings) is the VaPo protected against technical risks given by for a single accident year i:

period	instrument	cashflow	units
$t+1$	$Z^{(t+1)}$	$X_{t+1} \longrightarrow$	$l_{t+1}^*(i)$
$t+2$	$Z^{(t+2)}$	$X_{t+2} \longrightarrow$	$l_{t+2}^*(i)$
$\vdots$	$\vdots$	$\vdots$	$\vdots$
$t+k$	$Z^{(t+k)}$	$X_{t+k} \longrightarrow$	$l_{t+k}^*(i)$
$\vdots$	$\vdots$	$\vdots$	$\vdots$

where for $k \geq 1$

$$l_{t+k}^*(i) = \widehat{E_{t+k}^{(t)}}(i) + i \cdot \beta \cdot \widehat{E}\left[\left(X_{i,j^*(i)+k} - \widehat{E_{t+k}^{(t)}}(i)\right)^2 \middle| \mathcal{T}_t\right]^{1/2}. \tag{5.89}$$

Remarks.

- Now $l_{t+k}^*(i)$ covers both, risks coming from the stochastic process (process error) and uncertainties coming from the fact that we have to estimate parameters.
- **Pay attention** to the fact that we have not considered possible dependencies between the accounting years:
Indeed, $E_{t+k}^{(t)}(i)$ is estimated by

$$\widehat{E_{t+k}^{(t)}}(i) = C_{i,j^*(i)} \cdot \prod_{l=0}^{k-2} \widehat{f}_{j^*(i)+l} \cdot \left(\widehat{f}_{j^*(i)+k-1} - 1\right) \tag{5.90}$$

and $E^{(t)}_{t+k+1}(i)$ is estimated by

$$\widehat{E^{(t)}_{t+k+1}}(i) = C_{i,j^*(i)} \cdot \prod_{l=0}^{k-1} \widehat{f}_{j^*(i)+l} \cdot \left(\widehat{f}_{j^*(i)+k} - 1\right). \qquad (5.91)$$

Hence they use the same estimated age-to-age factors $\widehat{f}_j$, which means that the parameter errors are correlated. We will not further investigate this problem here, since in the next section we have the same problem, when we aggregate different accident years.

Example 5.1 (revisited).

For our example we calculate both the parameter error $\widetilde{V^{(t)}_{t+k}}(i)^{1/2}$ and the process error $\widehat{V^{(t)}_{t+k}}(i)^{1/2}$. For low development periods, the process error is the dominant term whereas for higher development periods they have about the same size (this comes from the fact that we have only little data to estimate late development factors).

Parameter error $\widetilde{V^{(t)}_{t+k}}(i)^{1/2}$.

	1	2	3	4	5	6	7	8	9	10
0										
1										57'628
2									56'970	57'055
3								27'163	56'151	56'199
4							87'733	25'353	51'975	51'565
5						102'068	92'721	27'334	55'408	54'296
6				99'925	113'519	103'131	30'954	62'123	60'182
7			151'271	122'620	137'303	124'760	38'833	76'414	72'259
8		82'715	131'364	104'103	115'123	104'622	33'562	65'004	60'188
9	75'503	92'152	130'499	97'599	104'075	94'627	32'962	61'279	53'294

Process error $\widehat{V^{(t)}_{t+k}}(i)^{1/2}$.

	1	2	3	4	5	6	7	8	9	10
0										
1										48'832
2									75'052	48'603
3								45'268	74'566	48'243
4							178'062	44'398	72'835	46'336
5						225'149	183'669	47'407	77'269	47'781
6				229'965	238'145	194'528	52'055	84'306	50'590
7			346'712	258'879	264'121	216'465	62'761	100'344	56'248
8		226'818	332'762	242'972	244'204	200'828	62'482	98'906	52'140
9	234'816	275'881	364'358	250'614	240'498	199'983	74'127	115'011	51'779

□

5.5.4 Aggregation of parameter risks across different accident years

We consider now the whole diagonal of our claims development trapezoids (see (5.38)). The expected accounting year payments

$$E_{t+k}^{(t)} = \sum_{i+j=t} C_{i,j} \cdot f_j \cdots f_{j+k-2} \cdot (f_{j+k-1} - 1) \qquad (5.92)$$

are estimated by

$$\widehat{E_{t+k}^{(t)}} = \sum_{i+j=t} C_{i,j} \cdot \widehat{f}_j \cdots \widehat{f}_{j+k-2} \cdot \left(\widehat{f}_{j+k-1} - 1 \right) = \sum_{i=0}^{I} \widehat{E_{t+k}^{(t)}}(i). \quad (5.93)$$

The conditional **mean square error of prediction** (MSEP) is now given by

$$E\left[\left(\sum_{i+j=t+k} X_{i,j} - \sum_{i} \widehat{E_{t+k}^{(t)}}(i) \right)^2 \middle| \mathcal{T}_t \right] \qquad (5.94)$$

$$= \sum_{i} \operatorname{Var}\left(X_{i,j^*(i)+k} \middle| \mathcal{T}_t \right) + \left(\sum_{i} E_{t+k}^{(t)}(i) - \widehat{E_{t+k}^{(t)}}(i) \right)^2$$

$$= \sum_{i} V_{t+k}^{(t)}(i) + \sum_{i} \left(E_{t+k}^{(t)}(i) - \widehat{E_{t+k}^{(t)}}(i) \right)^2$$

$$+ \sum_{i \neq m} \left(E_{t+k}^{(t)}(i) - \widehat{E_{t+k}^{(t)}}(i) \right) \left(E_{t+k}^{(t)}(m) - \widehat{E_{t+k}^{(t)}}(m) \right).$$

Hence the first two terms are estimated by (5.88), but now we obtain an additional (covariance) term

$$\sum_{i \neq m} \left(E_{t+k}^{(t)}(i) - \widehat{E_{t+k}^{(t)}}(i) \right) \left(E_{t+k}^{(t)}(m) - \widehat{E_{t+k}^{(t)}}(m) \right). \qquad (5.95)$$

As above we resample $\widehat{f}_j$ in the conditional version. Hence we choose again the conditional resampling measure $P_{\mathcal{B}_J}$ an estimate the covariance term by

$$E_{\mathcal{B}_J} \left[\left(E_{t+k}^{(t)}(i) - \widehat{E_{t+k}^{(t)}}(i) \right) \left(E_{t+k}^{(t)}(m) - \widehat{E_{t+k}^{(t)}}(m) \right) \right] = C_{i,j^*(i)} \cdot C_{m,j^*(m)}$$

$$\cdot E_{\mathcal{B}_J} \left[\left(\prod_{l=0}^{k-2} f_{j^*(i)+l} \cdot \left(f_{j^*(i)+k-1} - 1 \right) - \prod_{l=0}^{k-2} \widehat{f}_{j^*(i)+l} \cdot \left(\widehat{f}_{j^*(i)+k-1} - 1 \right) \right) \right.$$

$$\left. \cdot \left(\prod_{l=0}^{k-2} f_{j^*(m)+l} \cdot \left(f_{j^*(m)+k-1} - 1 \right) - \prod_{l=0}^{k-2} \widehat{f}_{j^*(m)+l} \cdot \left(\widehat{f}_{j^*(m)+k-1} - 1 \right) \right) \right].$$

$$(5.96)$$

It now depends on the choice of i, m, k whether the expression above is different from zero: W.l.o.g. we assume that $m > i$. If

$$j^*(m) + k - 1 < j^*(i) \quad \Longleftrightarrow \quad m - (k-1) > i \qquad (5.97)$$

then we only use different development factors for the estimation of $E_{t+k}^{(t)}(i)$ and $E_{t+k}^{(t)}(m)$. I.e. for this indices (5.96) is equal to zero.

Choose m such that $i < m < i + k$, and define

$$g_{i,k-2} = \prod_{l=0}^{k-2} f_{j^*(i)+l} \quad \text{and} \quad \widehat{g}_{i,k-2} = \prod_{l=0}^{k-2} \widehat{f}_{j^*(i)+l}. \qquad (5.98)$$

Hence the last term in (5.96) is

$$E_{\mathcal{B}_J}\left[\left(g_{i,k-2} \cdot \left(f_{j^*(i)+k-1} - 1\right) - \widehat{g}_{i,k-2} \cdot \left(\widehat{f}_{j^*(i)+k-1} - 1\right)\right)\right. \qquad (5.99)$$

$$\left. \cdot \left(g_{m,k-2} \cdot \left(f_{j^*(m)+k-1} - 1\right) - \widehat{g}_{m,k-2} \cdot \left(\widehat{f}_{j^*(m)+k-1} - 1\right)\right)\right]$$

$$= \mathrm{Cov}_{P_{\mathcal{B}_J}}\left(\widehat{g}_{i,k-2} \cdot \left(\widehat{f}_{j^*(i)+k-1} - 1\right), \widehat{g}_{m,k-2} \cdot \left(\widehat{f}_{j^*(m)+k-1} - 1\right)\right)$$

$$= E_{\mathcal{B}_J}\left[\widehat{g}_{i,k-2} \cdot \left(\widehat{f}_{j^*(i)+k-1} - 1\right) \cdot \widehat{g}_{m,k-2} \cdot \left(\widehat{f}_{j^*(m)+k-1} - 1\right)\right]$$

$$- g_{i,k-2} \cdot \left(f_{j^*(i)+k-1} - 1\right) \cdot g_{m,k-2} \cdot \left(f_{j^*(m)+k-1} - 1\right).$$

The first term on the r.h.s. of (5.99) is equal to

$$\prod_{l=j^*(m)}^{j^*(i)-1} f_l \cdot \prod_{l=j^*(i)}^{j^*(m)+k-2} E_{\mathcal{B}_J}\left[\widehat{f}_l^2\right] \qquad (5.100)$$

$$\cdot E_{\mathcal{B}_J}\left[\left(\widehat{f}_{j^*(m)+k-1} - 1\right) \cdot \widehat{f}_{j^*(m)+k-1}\right] \prod_{l=j^*(m)+k}^{j^*(i)+k-2} f_l \cdot \left(f_{j^*(i)+k-1} - 1\right).$$

This term is equal to

$$\prod_{l=j^*(m)}^{j^*(i)-1} f_l \cdot \prod_{l=j^*(i)}^{j^*(m)+k-2} \left(\frac{\sigma_l^2}{\sum_n C_{n,l}} + f_l^2\right)$$

$$\cdot \left(\frac{\sigma_{j^*(m)+k-1}^2}{\sum_n C_{n,j^*(m)+k-1}} + \left(f_{j^*(m)+k-1} - 1\right) \cdot f_{j^*(m)+k-1}\right) \qquad (5.101)$$

$$\cdot \prod_{l=j^*(m)+k}^{j^*(i)+k-2} f_l \cdot \left(f_{j^*(i)+k-1} - 1\right).$$

Collecting all the term, we obtain for the r.h.s. of (5.99)

$$
\prod_{l=j^*(m)}^{j^*(i)-1} f_l \cdot \left[\prod_{l=j^*(i)}^{j^*(m)+k-2} \left(\frac{\sigma_l^2}{\sum_n C_{n,l}} + f_l^2 \right) \right.
$$

$$
\cdot \left(\frac{\sigma_{j^*(m)+k-1}^2}{\sum_n C_{n,j^*(m)+k-1}} + \left(f_{j^*(m)+k-1} - 1 \right) \cdot f_{j^*(m)+k-1} \right) \qquad (5.102)
$$

$$
- \prod_{l=j^*(i)}^{j^*(m)+k-2} f_l^2 \cdot \left(\left(f_{j^*(m)+k-1} - 1 \right) \cdot f_{j^*(m)+k-1} \right) \right]
$$

$$
\cdot \prod_{l=j^*(m)+k}^{j^*(i)+k-2} f_l \cdot \left(f_{j^*(i)+k-1} - 1 \right).
$$

This leads to the following estimates of the covariance terms for $i < m < i+k$

$$
\widehat{E_{t+k}^{(t)}}(i) \cdot \widehat{E_{t+k}^{(t)}}(m) \cdot \left[\prod_{l=j^*(i)}^{j^*(m)+k-2} \left(\frac{\widehat{\sigma}_l^2 / \widehat{f}_l^2}{\sum_n C_{n,l}} + 1 \right) \right.
$$

$$
\cdot \left(\frac{\widehat{\sigma}_{j^*(m)+k-1}^2 / \left(\left(\widehat{f}_{j^*(m)+k-1} - 1 \right) \cdot \widehat{f}_{j^*(m)+k-1} \right)}{\sum_n C_{n,j^*(m)+k-1}} + 1 \right) - 1 \right].
$$

If we do a linear approximation (as above) we get

$$
\widetilde{V_{t+k}^{(t)}}(i,m) \stackrel{def.}{=} \widehat{E_{t+k}^{(t)}}(i) \cdot \widehat{E_{t+k}^{(t)}}(m) \qquad (5.103)
$$

$$
\cdot \left[\sum_{l=j^*(i)}^{j^*(m)+k-2} \frac{\widehat{\sigma}_l^2 / \widehat{f}_l^2}{\sum_n C_{n,l}} + \frac{\widehat{\sigma}_{j^*(m)+k-1}^2 / \left(\left(\widehat{f}_{j^*(m)+k-1} - 1 \right) \cdot \widehat{f}_{j^*(m)+k-1} \right)}{\sum_n C_{n,j^*(m)+k-1}} \right].
$$

Estimator 5.8 (Conditional MSEP) *The conditional mean square error of prediction for the accounting years is estimated by (see also (5.93))*

$$
\widehat{E} \left[\left(\sum_{i+j=t+k} X_{i,j} - \widehat{E_{t+k}^{(t)}} \right)^2 \Bigg| \mathcal{T}_t \right] \qquad (5.104)
$$

$$
= \sum_{i=0}^{I} \left(\widehat{V_{t+k}^{(t)}}(i) + \widetilde{V_{t+k}^{(t)}}(i) + 2 \cdot \sum_{m=i+1}^{i+k-1} \widetilde{V_{t+k}^{(t)}}(i,m) \right),
$$

where $\widehat{V_{t+k}^{(t)}}(i)$ is given in (5.68), $\widetilde{V_{t+k}^{(t)}}(i)$ is given in (5.87) and $\widetilde{V_{t+k}^{(t)}}(i,m)$ is given in (5.103).

Henceforth in the pragmatic approach (first version with standard devation loadings) is the VaPo protected against technical risks given by

period	instrument	cashflow	units
$t+1$	$Z^{(t+1)}$	X_{t+1} $\longrightarrow$	l^*_{t+1}
$t+2$	$Z^{(t+2)}$	X_{t+2} $\longrightarrow$	l^*_{t+2}
$\vdots$	$\vdots$	$\vdots$	$\vdots$
$t+k$	$Z^{(t+k)}$	X_{t+k} $\longrightarrow$	l^*_{t+k}
$\vdots$	$\vdots$	$\vdots$	$\vdots$

where for $k \geq 1$

$$l^*_{t+k} = \widehat{E^{(t)}_{t+k}} + i \cdot \beta \cdot \widehat{E}\left[\left(\sum_{i+j=t+k} X_{i,j} - \widehat{E^{(t)}_{t+k}}\right)^2 \Bigg| \mathcal{T}_t\right]^{1/2}. \qquad (5.105)$$

Remark. As above, our l^*_{t+k} gives now a protection against process and parameter errors. But so far it doesn't take into account that parameter errors for different accounting years are correlated. Hence in that sense, neglecting the dependencies between accounting years, we have still a simplified model.

Example 5.1 (revisited).
We obtain the following values for the parameter errors:
In the claims development triangle we give the individual parameter errors $\widetilde{V^{(t)}_{t+k}}(i)^{1/2}$, whereas the last column illustrates the square root of the aggregate covariance terms within the accounting years

$$\widetilde{\mathrm{Cov}}^{1/2} = \left(2 \cdot \sum_{i<m} \widetilde{V^{(t)}_{t+k}}(i,m)\right)^{1/2}. \qquad (5.106)$$

Hence we have:

	1	2	3	4	5	6	7	8	9	10	$\widetilde{\mathrm{Cov}}^{1/2}$
0											
1										57'628	0
2									56'970	57'055	133'023
3								27'163	56'151	56'199	151'288
4							87'733	25'353	51'975	51'565	135'535
5						102'068	92'721	27'334	55'408	54'296	112'891
6					99'925	113'519	103'131	30'954	62'123	60'182	77'669
7				151'271	122'620	137'303	124'760	38'833	76'414	72'259	38'802
8			82'715	131'364	104'103	115'123	104'622	33'562	65'004	60'188	19'970
9		75'503	92'152	130'499	97'599	104'075	94'627	32'962	61'279	53'294	0

Hence the estimated square root of the mean square error of prediction for accounting years $pe_k^{1/2} = \widehat{E}\left[\left(\sum_{i+j=t+k} X_{i,j} - \widehat{E_{t+k}^{(t)}}\right)^2 \middle| \mathcal{T}_t\right]^{1/2}$ and its estimated variatonal coefficients are given by

$t+k$	$t+1$	$t+2$	$t+3$	$t+4$	$t+5$	$t+6$	$t+7$	$t+8$	$t+9$
l_{t+k}	5'226'536	4'179'394	3'131'668	2'127'272	1'561'879	1'177'744	744'287	445'521	86'555
$pe_k^{1/2}$	665'562	664'239	629'383	493'486	392'859	286'530	174'586	154'022	74'305
vco	12.7%	15.9%	20.1%	23.2%	25.2%	24.3%	23.5%	34.6%	85.8%

We define the cost-of-capital charge as follows

$$\text{CoC}(k) = i \cdot \beta \cdot pe_k^{1/2}. \tag{5.107}$$

Of course, both $\text{CoC}(k)$ and $pe_k^{1/2}$ depend on t because for the parameter estimation we have used information $\mathcal{T}_t$.

The valuation portfolio protected against technical risks is defined as

$$l_{t+k}^* = l_{t+k} + \text{CoC}(k), \tag{5.108}$$

with $i = 8\%$ and $\beta = \Phi^{-1}(99\%)$. Then we obtain

$t+k$	$t+1$	$t+2$	$t+3$	$t+4$	$t+5$	$t+6$	$t+7$	$t+8$	$t+9$
CoC	123'866	123'620	117'133	91'842	73'114	53'326	32'492	28'665	13'829
l_{t+k}^*	5'350'402	4'303'015	3'248'801	2'219'113	1'634'993	1'231'069	776'779	474'186	100'383

Table 5.6. Valuation portfolio protected against technical risk (process error and parameter error)

Hence for the three different accounting principles (nominal, constant interest rate, risk free rates SST (see Table 5.2) we obtain (see also Tables 5.3 and 5.5):

	VaPo	VaPo^{prot}	difference
1) nominal	18'680'856	19'338'741	657'886
2) $r = 1.50\%$	17'873'967	18'497'998	624'031
3) SST rates	17'847'512	18'468'169	620'657

Table 5.7. Monetary value of the valuation portfolio protected against technical risks (process error and parameter error) for different accounting principles

□

5.6 Unallocated loss adjustment expenses

5.6.1 Motivation

In this section we describe the "New York"-method for the estimation of unallocated loss adjustment expenses (ULAE). The "New York"-method for estimating ULAE is found in the literature (e.g. as footnotes in [Fe03] and

[CAS90] and in more detail in [BBMW06b]). Sometimes this method is also called paid-to-paid method.

In non-life insurance there are usually two different kinds of claims handling costs, external ones and internal ones. External costs like costs for external lawyers or for an external expertise etc. are usually allocated to single claims and are therefore contained in the usual claims payments and loss development figures. These payments are called allocated loss adjustment expenses (ALAE). Typically, internal loss adjustment expenses (income of claims handling department, maintenance of claims handling system, internal lawyers, management fees, etc.) are not contained in the claims figures and therefore have to be estimated separately. These internal costs can usually not be allocated to single claims. We call these costs unallocated loss adjustment expenses (ULAE). From a regulatory point of view, we should also build reserves for these costs/expenses because they are part of the claims handling process which guarantees that an insurance company is able to meet all its obligations. I.e. ULAE reserves should guarantee the smooth runoff of the old insurance liabilities without a "pay-as-you-go" system from new business/premium.

Concluding this means that ULAE reserves should also be part of the valuation portfolio, if we want to have a self-financing runoff of an insurance portfolio.

5.6.2 Pure claims payments

Usually, claims development figures only consist of "pure" claims payments not containing ULAE charges. They are usually studied in loss development triangles or trapezoids as described above (see Section 5.5).

In this section we denote by $X_{i,j}^{(pure)}$ the "pure" incremental payments for accident year i ($0 \leq i \leq I$) in development year j ($1 \leq j \leq J$). "Pure" always means, that these sizes do not contain ULAE (this is exactly the quantity studied in Section 5.5). The cumulative pure payments for accident year i after development period j are denoted by (see (5.28))

$$C_{i,j}^{(pure)} = \sum_{k=1}^{j} X_{i,k}^{(pure)}. \tag{5.109}$$

We assume that $X_{i,j}^{(pure)} = 0$ for all $j > J$, i.e. the ultimate pure cumulative loss is given by $C_{i,J}^{(pure)}$.

We have observations for $\mathcal{T}_t = \{X_{i,j}^{(pure)} : 0 \leq i \leq I$ and $1 \leq j \leq \min\{J, t - i\}\}$ and the complement of $\mathcal{T}_t$ needs to be predicted.

For the New York-method we also need a second type of development trapezoids, namely a "reporting" trapezoid: For accident year i, $Z_{i,j}^{(pure)}$ denotes the pure cumulative ultimate claim amount for all those claims, which are reported up to (and including) development year j. Hence

$$\left(Z_{i,1}^{(pure)}, Z_{i,2}^{(pure)}, \dots \right) \qquad (5.110)$$

with $Z_{i,J}^{(pure)} = C_{i,J}^{(pure)}$ describes, how the pure ultimate claim $C_{i,J}^{(pure)}$ is reported over time at the insurance company. Of course, this reporting pattern is much more delicate, because claims which are reported in the upper set $\widetilde{\mathcal{D}}_t = \{Z_{i,j}^{(pure)} : 0 \leq i \leq I \text{ and } 1 \leq j \leq \min\{J, t - i\}\}$ are still developing, since usually it takes quite some time between the reporting and the final settlement of a claim. Hence, the claim sizes/severities in $\widetilde{\mathcal{D}}_t$ are still random variables, however, they are already reported and therefore we already have some information on these reported claims. In general, the final value for $Z_{i,j}^{(pure)}$ is only known at time $i + J$.

Remark. The New York-method has to be understood as an algorithm used to estimate expected ULAE payments. This algorithm is not based on a stochastic model. Therefore, we assume in this section that all our variables are **deterministic** numbers. Stochastic variables are replaced by their "best estimates" for its conditional mean at time t. We think that for the current presentation (to explain the New York-method) it is not helpful to work in a stochastic framework.

5.6.3 ULAE charges

The cumulative ULAE payments for accident year i until development period j are denoted by $C_{i,j}^{(ULAE)}$. And finally, the total cumulative payments (pure and ULAE) are denoted by

$$C_{i,j} = C_{i,j}^{(pure)} + C_{i,j}^{(ULAE)}. \qquad (5.111)$$

The cumulative ULAE payments $C_{i,j}^{(ULAE)}$ and the incremental ULAE charges

$$X_{i,j}^{(ULAE)} = C_{i,j}^{(ULAE)} - C_{i,j-1}^{(ULAE)} \qquad (5.112)$$

need to be estimated: The main difficulty, now in practice, is that for each accounting year $t \leq I$ we have only one aggregated observation

$$X_t^{(ULAE)} = \sum_{\substack{i+j=t \\ 1 \leq j \leq J}} X_{i,j}^{(ULAE)} \qquad \text{(sum over t-diagonal).} \qquad (5.113)$$

That is, ULAE payments are usually not available for single accident years but rather we have a position "Total ULAE Expenses" for each accounting year t (in general ULAE charges are contained in the position "Administrative Expenses" in the annual profit-and-loss statement).

The reason for having only aggregated observations per accounting year is that in general the claims handling department treats several claims from different accident years simultaneously. Only a activity-based cost allocation split then allocates these expenses to different accident years. Hence, for the estimation of future ULAE payments we need first to define an appropriate model in order to split the aggregated observations $X_t^{(ULAE)}$ into the different accident years $X_{i,j}^{(ULAE)}$.

5.6.4 New York-method

The New York-method assumes that one part of the ULAE charge is proportional to the claims registration (denote this proportion by $r \in [0,1]$) and the other part is proportional to the settlement (payments) of the claims (proportion $1 - r$).

Assumption 5.9 *There are two development patterns* $(\gamma_j)_{j=1,\dots,J}$ *and* $(\alpha_j)_{j=1,\dots,J}$ *with* $\gamma_j \geq 0$, $\alpha_j \geq 0$, *for all* j, *and* $\sum_{j=1}^{J} \gamma_j = \sum_{j=1}^{J} \alpha_j = 1$ *such that* **(cashflow or payout pattern)**

$$X_{i,j}^{(pure)} = \gamma_j \cdot C_{i,J}^{(pure)} \tag{5.114}$$

and **(reporting pattern)**

$$Z_{i,j}^{(pure)} = \sum_{l=1}^{j} \alpha_l \cdot C_{i,J}^{(pure)} \tag{5.115}$$

for all i *and* j.

Remarks.

- For simplicity we assume a deterministic framework.
- Equation (5.114) describes, how the pure ultimate claim $C_{i,J}^{(pure)}$ is paid over time. In fact γ_j gives the cash flow pattern for the pure ultimate claim $C_{i,J}^{(pure)}$. It can easily be seen that this payout model satisfies the classical chain ladder assumptions for cumulative payments. Therefore we propose that γ_j is estimated by the classical chain ladder factors f_j, see (5.40)

$$\widehat{\gamma}_j = \frac{1}{f_j \cdots f_{J-1}} \cdot \left(1 - \frac{1}{f_{j-1}}\right). \tag{5.116}$$

- The estimation of the claims reporting pattern α_j in (5.115) is more delicate. There are not many claims reserving methods which give a reporting pattern α_j. Such a pattern can only be obtained if one separates the claims estimates for reported claims and IBNyR claims (incurred but not yet reported).

Model 5.10 *Assume that there exists* $r \in [0,1]$ *such that the incremental ULAE payments satisfy for all* i *and all* j

$$X_{i,j}^{(ULAE)} = \left(r \cdot \alpha_j + (1-r) \cdot \gamma_j\right) \cdot C_{i,J}^{(ULAE)}. \tag{5.117}$$

Henceforth, we assume that one part (r) of the ULAE charge is proportional to the reporting pattern (one has loss adjustment expenses at the registration of the claim), and the other part $(1 - r)$ of the ULAE charge is proportional to the claims settlement (measured by the payout pattern).

Definition 5.11 (Paid-to-paid ratio) *We define for all t*

$$\pi_t = \frac{X_t^{(ULAE)}}{X_t^{(pure)}} = \frac{\sum\limits_{\substack{i+j=t \\ 1 \le j \le J}} X_{i,j}^{(ULAE)}}{\sum\limits_{\substack{i+j=t \\ 1 \le j \le J}} X_{i,j}^{(pure)}}. \tag{5.118}$$

The paid-to-paid ratio measures the ULAE payments relative to the pure claim payments in each accounting year t.

Lemma 5.7. *Assume there exists $\pi > 0$ such that for all accident years i we have*

$$\frac{C_{i,J}^{(ULAE)}}{C_{i,J}^{(pure)}} = \pi. \tag{5.119}$$

Under Assumption 5.9 and Model 5.10 we have for all accounting years t

$$\pi_t = \pi, \tag{5.120}$$

whenever $C_{i,J}^{(pure)}$ is constant in i.

Proof of Lemma 5.7. We have

$$\pi_t = \frac{\sum\limits_{\substack{i+j=t \\ 1 \le j \le J}} X_{i,j}^{(ULAE)}}{\sum\limits_{\substack{i+j=t \\ 1 \le j \le J}} X_{i,j}^{(pure)}} = \frac{\sum\limits_{j=1}^{J} \left(r \cdot \alpha_j + (1-r) \cdot \gamma_j \right) \cdot C_{t-j,J}^{(ULAE)}}{\sum\limits_{j=1}^{J} \gamma_j \cdot C_{t-j,J}^{(pure)}}$$

$$= \pi \cdot \frac{\sum\limits_{j=1}^{J} \left(r \cdot \alpha_j + (1-r) \cdot \gamma_j \right) \cdot C_{t-j,J}^{(pure)}}{\sum\limits_{j=1}^{J} \gamma_j \cdot C_{t-j,J}^{(pure)}} = \pi. \tag{5.121}$$

This finishes the proof.

$\square$

We define the following split of the claims reserves for accident year i at time j:

$$R_{i,j}^{(pure)} = \sum_{l>j} X_{i,l}^{(pure)} = \sum_{l>j} \gamma_l \cdot C_{i,J}^{(pure)} \text{ (total reserv. for pure future paym.)},$$

$$R_{i,j}^{(IBNR)} = \sum_{l>j} \alpha_l \cdot C_{i,J}^{(pure)} \text{ (IBNyR reserves, incurred but not yet reported)},$$

$$R_{i,j}^{(rep)} = R_{i,j}^{(pure)} - R_{i,j}^{(IBNR)} \quad \text{(reserves for reported claims)}.$$

Result 5.12 (New York-method) *Under the assumptions of Lemma 5.7 we can predict π using the observations π_t (accounting year data). The reserves for ULAE charges for accident year i after development year j, $R_{i,j}^{(ULAE)} = \sum_{l>j} X_{i,l}^{(ULAE)}$, are estimated by*

$$\widehat{R}_{i,j}^{(ULAE)} = \pi \cdot r \cdot R_{i,j}^{(IBNR)} + \pi \cdot (1 - r) \cdot R_{i,j}^{(pure)}$$

$$= \pi \cdot R_{i,j}^{(IBNR)} + \pi \cdot (1 - r) \cdot R_{i,j}^{(rep)}. \tag{5.122}$$

Explanation of Result 5.12.

We have under the assumptions of Lemma 5.7 for all i, j

$$R_{i,j}^{(ULAE)} = \sum_{l>j} \left(r \cdot \alpha_l + (1 - r) \cdot \gamma_l \right) \cdot C_{i,J}^{(ULAE)} \tag{5.123}$$

$$= \pi \cdot \sum_{l>j} \left(r \cdot \alpha_l + (1 - r) \cdot \gamma_l \right) C_{i,J}^{(pure)}$$

$$= \pi \cdot r \cdot R_{i,j}^{(IBNR)} + \pi \cdot (1 - r) \cdot R_{i,j}^{(pure)}.$$

Remarks.

- In practice one assumes the stationarity condition $\pi_t = \pi$ for all t. This implies that π can be estimated from the accounting data of the annual profit-and-loss statements. Pure claims payments are directly contained in the profit-and-loss statements, whereas ULAE payments are often contained in the administrative expenses. Hence one needs to divide this position into further subpositions (e.g. with the help of an activity-based cost allocation split).

- Result 5.12 gives an easy formula for estimating ULAE reserves. If we are interested into the total ULAE reserves after accounting year t we simply have

$$\widehat{R}_t^{(ULAE)} = \sum_{i+j=t} \widehat{R}_{i,j}^{(ULAE)} = \pi \cdot \sum_{i+j=t} R_{i,j}^{(IBNR)} + \pi \cdot (1 - r) \cdot \sum_{i+j=t} R_{i,j}^{(rep)}, \tag{5.124}$$

i.e. all we need to know is, how to split the total pure claims reserves into reserves for IBNyR claims and reserves for reported claims.

- The assumptions for the New York-method are rather restrictive in the sense that the pure cumulative ultimate claim $C_{i,J}^{(pure)}$ must be constant in i (see Lemma 5.7). Otherwise the paid-to-paid ratio π_t for accounting years is not the same as the ratio $C_{i,J}^{(ULAE)}/C_{i,J}^{(pure)}$ even if the latter is assumed to be constant. Of course in practice the assumption of equal pure cumulative ultimate claim is never fulfilled. If we relax this condition we obtain the following lemma.

Lemma 5.8. *Assume there exists $\pi > 0$ such that for all accident years i we have*

$$\frac{C_{i,J}^{(ULAE)}}{C_{i,J}^{(pure)}} = \pi \cdot \left(r \cdot \frac{\overline{\alpha}}{\overline{\gamma}} + (1-r) \right)^{-1}, \tag{5.125}$$

with

$$\overline{\gamma} = \frac{\sum_{j=1}^{J} \gamma_j \cdot C_{t-j,J}^{(pure)}}{\sum_{j=1}^{J} C_{t-j,J}^{(pure)}} \qquad and \qquad \overline{\alpha} = \frac{\sum_{j=1}^{J} \alpha_j \cdot C_{t-j,J}^{(pure)}}{\sum_{j=1}^{J} C_{t-j,J}^{(pure)}}. \tag{5.126}$$

Under Assumption 5.9 and Model 5.10 we have for all accounting years t

$$\pi_t = \pi. \tag{5.127}$$

Proof of Lemma 5.8. As in Lemma 5.7 we obtain

$$\pi_t = \pi \cdot \left(r \cdot \frac{\overline{\alpha}}{\overline{\gamma}} + (1-r) \right)^{-1} \cdot \frac{\sum_{j=1}^{J} \left(r \cdot \alpha_j + (1-r) \cdot \gamma_j \right) \cdot C_{t-j,J}^{(pure)}}{\sum_{j=1}^{J} \gamma_j \cdot C_{t-j,J}^{(pure)}} = \pi. \tag{5.128}$$

This finishes the proof.

$\square$

Remarks.

- If all pure cumulative ultimates are equal then $\overline{\gamma} = \overline{\alpha} = 1/J$ (apply Lemma 5.7).
- Assume that there exists a constant $i^{(p)} > 0$ such that for all $i \geq 0$ we have $C_{i+1,J}^{(pure)} = (1 + i^{(p)}) \cdot C_{i,J}^{(pure)}$, i.e. constant growth $i^{(p)}$. If we blindly apply (5.120) of Lemma 5.7 (i.e. we do not apply the correction factor in (5.125)) and estimate the incremental ULAE payments by (5.122) and (5.124) we obtain

$$\sum_{i+j=t} \widehat{X}_{i,j}^{(ULAE)}$$

$$\overset{def.}{=} \pi \cdot \sum_{j=1}^{J} \left(r \cdot \alpha_j + (1-r) \cdot \gamma_j \right) \cdot C_{t-j,J}^{(pure)}$$

$$= \frac{X_t^{(ULAE)}}{X_t^{(pure)}} \cdot \sum_{j=1}^{J} \left(r \cdot \alpha_j + (1-r) \cdot \gamma_j \right) \cdot C_{t-j,J}^{(pure)} \tag{5.129}$$

$$= \sum_{i+j=t} X_{i,j}^{(ULAE)} \cdot \left(r \cdot \frac{\overline{\alpha}}{\overline{\gamma}} + (1-r) \right)$$

$$= \sum_{i+j=t} X_{i,j}^{(ULAE)} \cdot \left(r \cdot \frac{\sum_{j=1}^{J} \alpha_j \cdot \left(1 + i^{(p)} \right)^{J-j}}{\sum_{j=1}^{J} \gamma_j \cdot \left(1 + i^{(p)} \right)^{J-j}} + (1-r) \right)$$

$$> \sum_{i+j=t} X_{i,j}^{(ULAE)},$$

where the last inequality in general holds true for $i^{(p)} > 0$, since usually $(\alpha_j)_j$ is more concentrated than $(\gamma_j)_j$, i.e. we usually have $J > 1$ and

$$\sum_{l=1}^{j} \alpha_l > \sum_{l=1}^{j} \gamma_l \quad \text{for } j = 0, \ldots, J - 1. \tag{5.130}$$

This comes from the fact that the claims are reported before they are paid. I.e. if we blindly apply the New York-method for constant positive growth then the ULAE reserves are too high (for constant negative growth we obtain the opposite sign). This implies that we have always a positive loss experience on ULAE reserves for constant positive growth.

5.6.5 Example

We assume that the observations for π_t are generated by i.i.d. random variables $\frac{X_t^{(ULAE)}}{X_t^{(pure)}}$. Hence we can estimate π from this sequence. Assume $\pi = 10\%$. Moreover $i^{(p)} = 0$ and set $r = 50\%$ (this is the usual choice, also done in the SST [SST06]). Moreover we assume that we have the following reporting and cash flow patterns ($J = 5$):

$$(\alpha_1, \ldots, \alpha_5) = (90\%, 10\%, 0\%, 0\%, 0\%), \tag{5.131}$$
$$(\gamma_1, \ldots, \gamma_5) = (30\%, 20\%, 20\%, 20\%, 10\%). \tag{5.132}$$

Assume that $C_{i,J}^{(pure)} = 1'000$. Then the ULAE reserves for accident year i are given by

$$\left(\widehat{R}_{i,0}^{(ULAE)}, \ldots, \widehat{R}_{i,4}^{(ULAE)} \right) = (100, 40, 25, 15, 5), \tag{5.133}$$

which implies for the estimated incremental ULAE payments

$$\left(\widehat{X}_{i,1}^{(ULAE)}, \ldots, \widehat{X}_{i,5}^{(ULAE)} \right) = (60, 15, 10, 10, 5). \tag{5.134}$$

Hence for the total estimated payments $\widehat{X}_{i,j} = X_{i,j}^{(pure)} + \widehat{X}_{i,j}^{(ULAE)}$ we have

$$\left(\widehat{X}_{i,1}, \ldots, \widehat{X}_{i,5} \right) = (360, 215, 210, 210, 105). \tag{5.135}$$

5.7 Conclusion on the non-life VaPo

We have constructed both the Valuation Portfolio and the Valuation Portfolio protected against technical risks for a runoff portfolio of a non-life insurance company. In fact our solution is only a first approach to the construction of an appropriate replicating portfolio for a non-life insurance portfolio.

Open problems for example are:

• Appropriate choice of the financial basis, such that we have an independent decoupling into insurance technical risks and financial risks.

- Choice of an appropriate risk measure which also takes into account the dependencies between accounting years.
- Make an appropriate choice for the cost-of-capital rate.
- Choose an appropriate stochastic claims reserving model in order to determine claims reserves, cashflow patterns, uncertainties in the estimates and predictions, etc.
- Here we have only treated the run-off situation of a non-life insurance portfolio. The premium liability risk could, theoretically, also be put into our framework, by assuming that $C_{I,0} = -\Pi_I$. However, this approach does often not lead to good estimates for the premium liabilities and premium liability risks. We therefore recommend to rather treat the premium liability risk in a separate model (such as it is done in almost all risk adjusted solvency calculations).

In this separate model, premium liability risks are often split into two categories: i) small (single) claims, ii) large single claims, or cumulative events (such as hailstorms, floods, etc.) (see e.g. SST [SST06]).

The main risk in i) is, that the prediction of future parameters may have large uncertainties. This can be modelled assuming that true future parameters are latent variables which we try to predict (see e.g. [Wü06b]).

The risks in class ii) are often modelled using a compound model (for low frequencies and high severities). One main difficulty in this class of risks is to estimate the parameters, because usually one has only little information. We propose to use internal data, external data and expert opinion for the estimation of the parameters. This can e.g. be done in a Bayesian or credibility framework, similarly as it is done for operational risks in the banking industry (see e.g. [BSW07] and [SW06]).

6

Selected Topics

We conclude these lecture notes with some selected topics and remarks. These remarks are rather unstructured. They give some ideas that go beyond the presentations of the previous chapters. In general, we believe that still a lot of work, developments and research has to be done in order to come to a unified market-consistent valuation approach that respects economic intuition, financial mathematics and actuarial sciences.

6.1 Sources of losses and profits, profit sharing

We denote by $\mathbf{X} = (X_{T+1}, X_{T+2}, \ldots)$ the cashflows after time T of **all contracts** which are in force at time T. Hence the valuation portfolio at time T of our business is given by (see Section 3.6).

$$\text{VaPo}_{(T)}(\mathbf{X}) = \sum_{t>T} \text{VaPo}_{(T)}(\mathbf{X}_t) = \sum_{t>T} \sum_{i=1}^{p} l_{i,t}^{(T)} \cdot \mathcal{U}_i, \qquad (6.1)$$

with $\mathbf{X}_t = X_t \cdot \mathbf{Z}^{(t)}$, $(\mathcal{U}_i)_{i=1,\ldots p}$ are the units (basis, financial instruments) and

$$l_{i,t}^{(T)} = E\left[\Lambda_i(\mathbf{X}_t)|\,\mathcal{T}_T\right] \qquad (6.2)$$

denotes the expected number of units $\mathcal{U}_i$ generated by the stochastic cash flow $\mathbf{X}_t$ (seen from time T). Similarly, we can define

$$\text{VaPo}_{(T+1)}(\mathbf{X}) = \sum_{t>T} \text{VaPo}_{(T+1)}(\mathbf{X}_t) = \sum_{t>T} \sum_{i=1}^{p} l_{i,t}^{(T+1)} \cdot \mathcal{U}_i. \qquad (6.3)$$

Hence $\text{VaPo}_{(T)}(\mathbf{X})$ is $\mathcal{T}_T$-measurable and $\text{VaPo}_{(T+1)}(\mathbf{X})$ is $\mathcal{T}_{T+1}$-measurable. Moreover, by applying conditional expectations iteratively,

$$\text{VaPo}_{(T)}(\mathbf{X}) = E\left[\text{VaPo}_{(T+1)}(\mathbf{X})|\,\mathcal{T}_T\right] \qquad (6.4)$$

is the valuation portfolio seen at time T. Due to our construction we have the following recursion (linearity)

$$\text{VaPo}_{(T)}\left(\mathbf{X}\right) = E\left[\text{VaPo}_{(T+1)}\left(\mathbf{X}_{(T+2)}\right)\middle|\, \mathcal{T}_T\right] + E\left[\text{VaPo}_{(T+1)}\left(\mathbf{X}_{T+1}\right)\middle|\, \mathcal{T}_T\right]. \tag{6.5}$$

This is the self-financing property for stochastic cash flows (for deterministic cash flows see Section 3.4).

$\text{VaPo}_{(T+1)}\left(\mathbf{X}_{T+1}\right)$ is simply cash value at time $T+1$ ($\mathcal{F}_{T+1}$-measurable). Hence it is replaced by X_{T+1}. This leads to the recursion (at time $T+1$)

$$\text{VaPo}_{(T)}\left(\mathbf{X}\right) = E\left[\text{VaPo}_{(T+1)}\left(\mathbf{X}_{(T+2)}\right)\middle|\, \mathcal{T}_T\right] + E\left[X_{T+1}\middle|\, \mathcal{T}_T\right]. \tag{6.6}$$

Therefore the **technical loss** in the interval $(T, T+1]$ at time $T+1$ is given by

$$\begin{aligned}
&\text{VaPo}_{(T+1)}\left(\mathbf{X}_{(T+2)}\right) + X_{T+1} - \text{VaPo}_{(T)}\left(\mathbf{X}\right) \tag{6.7}\\
&= \text{VaPo}_{(T+1)}\left(\mathbf{X}_{(T+2)}\right) + X_{T+1}\\
&\qquad -E\left[\text{VaPo}_{(T+1)}\left(\mathbf{X}_{(T+2)}\right)\middle|\, \mathcal{T}_T\right] - E\left[X_{T+1}\middle|\, \mathcal{T}_T\right]\\
&= \text{VaPo}_{(T+1)}\left(\mathbf{X}_{(T+2)}\right) - E\left[\text{VaPo}_{(T+1)}\left(\mathbf{X}_{(T+2)}\right)\middle|\, \mathcal{T}_T\right]\\
&\qquad +X_{T+1} - E\left[X_{T+1}\middle|\, \mathcal{T}_T\right].
\end{aligned}$$

Hence the technical loss has two parts:

1. prediction error in the next payment, which is given by (at time $T+1$)

$$X_{T+1} - E\left[X_{T+1}\middle|\, \mathcal{T}_T\right], \tag{6.8}$$

2. prediction error in the valuation portfolio for cash flows after $T+1$, which is given by

$$\text{VaPo}_{(T+1)}\left(\mathbf{X}_{(T+2)}\right) - E\left[\text{VaPo}_{(T+1)}\left(\mathbf{X}_{(T+2)}\right)\middle|\, \mathcal{T}_T\right]. \tag{6.9}$$

Note that we predict random variables by its (conditional) expectations. Henceforth, the error terms are called prediction errors. If we, moreover, estimate the conditional expectations

$$E\left[X_{T+1}\middle|\, \mathcal{T}_T\right] \quad \text{and} \quad E\left[\text{VaPo}_{(T+1)}\left(\mathbf{X}_{(T+2)}\right)\middle|\, \mathcal{T}_T\right] \tag{6.10}$$

with the data available, we obtain an additional error term. Namely, the parameter estimation error term that comes from the fact the true mean is not known and estimated from data (this is completely analogous to the derivations in Chapter 5). Hence, in general, we have these two different sources of uncertainty.

For both error terms in (6.8)-(6.9) we have calculated a loading in the valuation protfolio protected against technical risks. Observe that the two error terms are not necessarily independent (see Section 3.5).

For the **financial loss** we proceed as follows: We have chosen an asset portfolio $\tilde{S}$ which fulfills the accounting condition at time T

$$\mathcal{E}_T\left[\mathrm{VaPo}_{(T)}(\mathbf{X})\right] = \mathcal{E}_T\left[\tilde{S}\right]. \tag{6.11}$$

We have a financial gain at time $T+1$ if

$$\mathcal{E}_{T+1}\left[\mathrm{VaPo}_{(T)}(\mathbf{X})\right] < \mathcal{E}_{T+1}\left[\tilde{S}\right], \tag{6.12}$$

and a financial loss otherwise.

If the portfolio is protected against financial risks we have no loss (we exercise the Margrabe option in case of a loss) but a gain if (6.12) holds.

Both, technical part and financial part may (and will) produce losses and gains:

1. If we have a protected portfolio, the gains should be shared by those who pay the protection fee.
2. If we have no protection, gains and losses should be shared in the same fixed proportion.

Other sources of risks: Model risks, credit risks, operational risks, etc. For a more detailed discussion of other risks we refer to [Sa06].

6.2 Remarks on the self-financing property

a) If we have a cash flow $\mathbf{X}$ with deterministic technical risk we construct a valuation portfolio

$$\mathbf{X} \mapsto \mathrm{VaPo}(\mathbf{X}) = \sum_i \lambda_i(\mathbf{X}) \cdot \mathcal{U}_i, \tag{6.13}$$

where the deterministic numbers $\lambda_i(\mathbf{X})$ are given in a natural way. As in Section 3.4 we then easily obtain the self-financing property (see Lemma 3.2)

$$\mathrm{VaPo}\left(\mathbf{X}_{(k)}\right) = \mathrm{VaPo}\left(\mathbf{X}_{(k+1)}\right) + \mathrm{VaPo}\left(\mathbf{X}_k\right). \tag{6.14}$$

Remark. Both sides of (6.14) should be read as portfolios.

b) If the cash flow $\mathbf{X}$ has stochastic technical risks, the situation is more complicated. In that case we have chosen for the valuation portfolio construction the expected number of units $\mathcal{U}_i$ (at time k)

$$l_i^{(k)}(\mathbf{X}) = E\left[\Lambda_i(\mathbf{X})\vert\, \mathcal{T}_k\right] \tag{6.15}$$

and then the valuation portfolio at time k is given by

$$\mathbf{X} \mapsto \mathrm{VaPo}_{(k)}(\mathbf{X}) = \sum_i l_i^{(k)}(\mathbf{X}) \cdot \mathcal{U}_i. \tag{6.16}$$

This valuation portfolio has the **self-financing property in the mean**. We have

$$l_i^{(k)}(\mathbf{X}) = E\left[l_i^{(k+1)}(\mathbf{X}) \middle| \mathcal{T}_k \right], \tag{6.17}$$

which implies the self-financing property in the mean as equation of the portfolios below (see also (6.5))

$$\begin{aligned}
\mathrm{VaPo}_{(k)}\left(\mathbf{X}_{(k)}\right) &= \mathrm{VaPo}_{(k)}\left(\mathbf{X}_{(k+1)}\right) + \mathrm{VaPo}_{(k)}\left(\mathbf{X}_k\right) \tag{6.18} \\
&= E\left[\mathrm{VaPo}_{(k+1)}\left(\mathbf{X}_{(k+1)}\right) \middle| \mathcal{T}_k \right] + \mathrm{VaPo}_{(k)}\left(\mathbf{X}_k\right).
\end{aligned}$$

c) Assume we have a cash flow $\mathbf{X}$ with stochastic technical risks and we consider the valuation portfolio protected against technical risks

$$\mathbf{X} \mapsto \mathrm{VaPo}_{(k)}^{prot}(\mathbf{X}) = \sum_i l_i^{*,k}(\mathbf{X}) \cdot \mathcal{U}_i, \tag{6.19}$$

with the "distortion representation" (see also (2.82))

$$l_i^{*,k}(\mathbf{X}) = E\left[\sum_t \varphi_t^{\mathcal{T}} \cdot \Lambda_i(\mathbf{X}_t) \middle| \mathcal{T}_k \right]. \tag{6.20}$$

In order to have a self-financing property we need that

$$l_i^{*,k}(\mathbf{X}) = E\left[l_i^{*,k+1}(\mathbf{X}) \middle| \mathcal{T}_k \right], \tag{6.21}$$

which follows from the distortion representation. Hence we have again the self-financing property in the mean as portfolio

$$\begin{aligned}
\mathrm{VaPo}_{(k)}^{prot}\left(\mathbf{X}_{(k)}\right) &= \mathrm{VaPo}_{(k)}^{prot}\left(\mathbf{X}_{(k+1)}\right) + \mathrm{VaPo}_{(k)}^{prot}\left(\mathbf{X}_k\right) \tag{6.22} \\
&= E\left[\mathrm{VaPo}_{(k+1)}^{prot}\left(\mathbf{X}_{(k+1)}\right) \middle| \mathcal{T}_k \right] + \mathrm{VaPo}_{(k)}^{prot}\left(\mathbf{X}_k\right).
\end{aligned}$$

Distortion techniques are used quite often in actuarial practice, e.g. in life insurance when one replaces the "best estimate" life table by a prudent life table. However, the loadings for technical risks are often not naturally obtained via a distortion as in (6.20). An example was given in Chapter 5. In such cases the self-financing property in case c) is replaced by
Self-financing property as portfolio

$$\sum_i l_i^{*,k}(\mathbf{X}_{(k)}) \cdot \mathcal{U}_i \ge \sum_i E\left[l_i^{*,k+1}(\mathbf{X}_{(k+1)}) \cdot \middle| \mathcal{T}_k \right] \cdot \mathcal{U}_i + X_k \cdot \mathcal{U}_0, \tag{6.23}$$

if $\mathcal{U}_0$ stand for the financial instrument representing cash value at time k. This means that in general we assume

$$l_i^{*,k}(\mathbf{X}) \geq E\left[l_i^{*,k+1}(\mathbf{X})\Big|\mathcal{T}_k\right]. \tag{6.24}$$

Self-financing property as monetary value. Assume that the price process $\mathcal{A}_s(\mathcal{U}_i)$ is independent of $\mathcal{T}$ and satisfies (4.9). The monetary value at time k of our protected VaPo is given by

$$\mathcal{A}_k\left(\mathrm{VaPo}_{(k)}^{prot}\left(\mathbf{X}_{(k)}\right)\right) = \sum_i l_i^{*,k}(\mathbf{X}_{(k)}) \cdot \mathcal{A}_k(\mathcal{U}_i), \tag{6.25}$$

and due to the independence of technical and financial risks, and because of (6.24)

$$E\left[\varphi_{k+1}^{(\mathcal{G})} \cdot \mathcal{A}_{k+1}\left(\mathrm{VaPo}_{(k+1)}^{prot}\left(\mathbf{X}_{(k+1)}\right)\right)\Big|\mathcal{F}_k\right]$$

$$= E\left[\varphi_{k+1}^{(\mathcal{G})} \cdot \sum_i l_i^{*,k+1}(\mathbf{X}_{(k+1)}) \cdot \mathcal{A}_{k+1}(\mathcal{U}_i)\Big|\mathcal{F}_k\right]$$

$$= \sum_i E\left[l_i^{*,k+1}(\mathbf{X}_{(k+1)})\Big|\mathcal{T}_k\right] \cdot E\left[\varphi_{k+1}^{(\mathcal{G})} \cdot \mathcal{A}_{k+1}(\mathcal{U}_i)\Big|\mathcal{G}_k\right]$$

$$\leq \sum_i l_i^{*,k}(\mathbf{X}_{(k+1)}) \cdot \varphi_k^{(\mathcal{G})} \cdot \mathcal{A}_k(\mathcal{U}_i). \tag{6.26}$$

This implies the self-financing property also in monetary value

$$E\left[\frac{\varphi_{k+1}^{(\mathcal{G})}}{\varphi_k^{(\mathcal{G})}} \cdot \mathcal{A}_{k+1}\left(\mathrm{VaPo}_{(k+1)}^{prot}\left(\mathbf{X}_{(k+1)}\right)\right)\Big|\mathcal{F}_k\right] \leq \mathcal{A}_k\left(\mathrm{VaPo}_{(k)}^{prot}\left(\mathbf{X}_{(k+1)}\right)\right). \tag{6.27}$$

This means that we obtain a super-martingale for the monetary value of the valuation portfolio protected against technical risks. Note that it is not straightforward that the super-martingale property is satisfied if we use ad-hoc methods for the calculation of the protection margin, e.g. the derivations in Chapter 5 do not necessarily lead to a self-financing valuation portfolio protected against technical risks.

6.3 Legal quote in life insurance

For the moment we consider only financial losses and gains, i.e. we assume a deterministic "best estimate" life table. Assume we have a technical interest rate i. We denote the yield of $\widetilde{S}$ in $[t, t+1]$ by R_{t+1}. We define the following rates of participations ($\beta \in [0, 1]$ denotes the legal quote)

$$\rho_{t+1}^{(1)} = \frac{\max\left(\beta \cdot R_{t+1}, i\right) - i}{1 + i}, \tag{6.28}$$

$$\rho_{t+1}^{(2)} = \beta \cdot \frac{\max\left(R_{t+1}, i\right) - i}{1 + i}. \tag{6.29}$$

Definition (6.28) can be viewed as a net legal quote, whereas (6.29) is rather a gross legal quote.

Remark. There are different ways to think about profit sharing. The easiest ways probably are

- cash bonus paid to the policyholder,
- (in practice) transfer into final cash bonus (for single premium policies one increases the sum insured by $\rho_{t+1}^{(k)}$, $k = 1, 2$).

Example 6.1 (Purely theoretical).

Choose a pure endowment policy with a duration of 20 years and a single premium. In this example we assume that there is no mortality ($\Rightarrow$ only financial risk) and that the sum insured is 100. For an other example we refer to De Felice-Moriconi [dFM04].

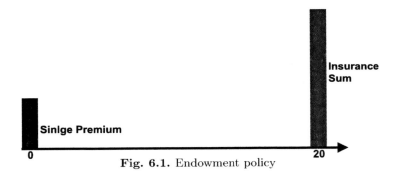

Fig. 6.1. Endowment policy

The valuation portfolio is given by (the basis is the zero coupon bond $Z^{(20)}$)

$$\text{VaPo} = 100 \cdot Z^{(20)}. \tag{6.30}$$

The monetary actuarial value if we take constant interest rate $i = 3\%$ is given by

$$\mathcal{A}_0 \left[\text{VaPo}\right] = 100 \cdot (1 + i)^{-20} = 55.37, \tag{6.31}$$
$$\mathcal{A}_t \left[\text{VaPo}\right] = 100 \cdot (1 + i)^{-(20-t)}. \tag{6.32}$$

The economic value is given by

$$V_t = \mathcal{E}_t \left[\text{VaPo}\right] = 100 \cdot \mathcal{E}_t \left[Z^{(20)}\right]. \tag{6.33}$$

On the other hand we have an investment portfolio $\widetilde{S}$ with

$$Y_t = \mathcal{E}_t \left[\widetilde{S}\right], \tag{6.34}$$

which determines the participation benefits. We consider an example with annual volatility of $\widetilde{Y}_t = Y_t/V_t$ of $\sigma = 4\%$ and participation rate $\beta = 100\%$ (see also Subsection 4.3.2).

The benefit is paid by increasing the sum insured each year by $\rho_s^{(k)}$. Hence the final sum insured (viewed from time 0) is

$$100 \cdot \prod_{s=1}^{20} \left(1 + \rho_s^{(k)}\right) = 100 \cdot \phi_0^{(20)}, \tag{6.35}$$

where

$$\phi_0^{(20)} \quad \text{is a stochastic "zero coupon bond" at time 0,} \tag{6.36}$$
$$Z^{(20)} \quad \text{is the standard zero coupon bond.} \tag{6.37}$$

If we think now of paying the legal quote to the insured we obtain the following valuation portfolio at time $t < 20$

$$\text{VaPo}_t^{lq} = 100 \cdot \prod_{s=t+1}^{20} \left(1 + \rho_s^{(k)}\right) = 100 \cdot \phi_t^{(20)}. \tag{6.38}$$

Hence the valuation portfolio and the valuation portfolio with legal quote at time $t < 20$ are given by

$$\text{VaPo} = 100 \cdot Z^{(20)} \quad \text{with} \quad \mathcal{E}_t\left[\text{VaPo}\right] = 100 \cdot \mathcal{E}_t\left[Z^{(20)}\right], \tag{6.39}$$

$$\text{VaPo}_t^{lq} = 100 \cdot \phi_t^{(20)} \quad \text{with} \quad \mathcal{E}_t\left[\text{VaPo}_t^{lq}\right] = 100 \cdot \mathcal{E}_t\left[\phi_t^{(20)}\right]. \tag{6.40}$$

For a specific example we obtain the following data: We use real Italian market data (which had very high yields initially), to determine the monetary value Monte Carlo simulations were used. From a shareholder's point of view one obtains Table 6.1.

One can also calculate a put decomposition: Define

$$100 \cdot \widetilde{\phi}_t^{(20)} = 100 \cdot \prod_{s=t+1}^{20} \left(1 + \frac{\beta \cdot R_s - i}{1+i}\right), \tag{6.41}$$

i.e. no guaranteed minimal interest rate i. Hence we can understand

$$\mathcal{E}_t\left[\text{VaPo}_t^{lq}\right] = 100 \cdot \mathcal{E}_t\left[\phi_t^{(20)}\right] = 100 \cdot \left(\mathcal{E}_t\left[\widetilde{\phi}_t^{(20)}\right] + \text{Put}_t\right). \tag{6.42}$$

Remarks.

- The reserves $\mathcal{E}_t\left[\text{VaPo}_t^{lq}\right]$ in this example are **not** reserves in the actuarial sense and can **not** be used for solvency purposes.

t	$\mathcal{A}_t\,[\text{VaPo}]$	$\mathcal{E}_t\,[\text{VaPo}]$	$\mathcal{E}_t\left[\text{VaPo}_t^{lq}\right]$	Call_t
0	55.37	5.60	33.00	27.40
1	57.03	6.81	35.13	28.32
2	58.74	11.49	39.63	28.14
3	60.50	12.09	41.20	29.11
4	62.32	24.71	49.59	24.88
5	64.19	16.63	46.82	30.19
6	66.11	23.02	50.88	27.86
7	68.10	36.90	59.23	22.33
8	70.14	50.25	67.35	17.10
9	72.24	61.82	76.33	14.51
10	74.41	56.58	71.99	15.41
11	76.64	61.62	73.56	11.94
12	78.94	66.71	76.06	9.35
13	81.31	75.25	81.31	6.06
14	83.75	79.30	84.38	5.08

Table 6.1. Calculations by courtesy of De Felice-Moriconi. For a description of their method we refer to [dFM04].

- E.g. for going from $\mathcal{E}_8\left[\text{VaPo}_8^{lq}\right] = 67.35$ to $\mathcal{E}_9\left[\text{VaPo}_9^{lq}\right] = 76.33$ we need an investment return of 13.3%. But the legal quote caps our return at $i = 3\%$!
- Using $\mathcal{E}_t\left[\text{VaPo}_t^{lq}\right]$ leads to the wrong reasoning
  - The market value accounting principle $\mathcal{E}_t$ is here not applicable.
  - The participations given to the insured caps the returns available for reserve accumulation, hence we can not apply $\mathcal{E}_t$.
- Correct reasoning: For policies with β-participation $\rho_t^{(2)}$ make two policies: Policy 1) for insured amount $\times\,\beta$; Policy 2) for insured amount $\times\,1-\beta$.
  - For Policy 1) we need statutory reserves with discount rate i and a put option for the minimum interest rate guarantee.
  - For Policy 2) we have economic reserves with a put option for minimum interest rate guarantee.

References

[BBK04]   Baumgartner, G., Bühlmann, H., Koller, M. (2004). Multidimensional valuation of life insurance policies and fair value. Bulletin SAA, 2004/1, 27-64.

[BBMW05]   Buchwalder, M., Bühlmann H., Merz, M., Wüthrich, M.V. (2005). Legal valuation portfolio in non-life insurance. Conference paper presented at the 36th Int. ASTIN Colloquium, 4-7 September 2005, ETH Zürich.

[BBMW06a] Buchwalder, M., Bühlmann H., Merz, M., Wüthrich, M.V. (2006). The mean square error of prediction in the chain ladder reserving method (Mack and Murphy revisited). ASTIN Bulletin 36/2, 521-542.

[BBMW06b] Buchwalder, M., Bühlmann H., Merz, M., Wüthrich, M.V. (2006). Estimation of unallocated loss adjustment expenses. Bulletin SAA, 2006/1, 43-53.

[BBMW07]   Buchwalder, M., Bühlmann H., Merz, M., Wüthrich, M.V. (2007). Valuation portfolio in non-life insurance. Scand. Act. J., 2007/2, 108-125.

[Bü92]   Bühlmann, H. (1992). Stochastic discounting. Insurance: Math. Econom. 11, 113-127.

[Bü95]   Bühlmann, H. (1995). Life insurance with stochastic interest rates. In: Financial Risk in Insurance, G. Ottaviani (Ed.), Springer.

[Bü04]   Bühlmann, H. (2004). Multidimensional valuation. Finance 25, 15-29.

[BDES98]   Bühlmann, H., Delbaen, F., Embrechts, P., Shiryaev, A. N. (1998). On the Esscher transform in discrete finance models, ASTIN Bulletin 28/2, 171-186.

[BSW07]   Bühlmann, H., Shevchenko, P.V., Wüthrich, M.V. (2007). A "toy" model for operational risk quantification using credibility theory. J. OpRisk 2/1, 3-19.

[CAS90]   Casualty Actuarial Society (CAS) (1990). Foundations of Casualty Actuarial Science, fourth edition.

[Co01]   Cochrane, J.H. (2001). Asset Pricing. Princeton University Press, Princeton and Oxford.

[dFM04]   De Felice, M., Moriconi, F. (2004). Market consistent valuation in life insurance. Measuring fair value and embedded options. Giornale dell'Istituto Italiano degli Attuari, VLXVII, Roma, 95-117.

[DS94]   Delbaen, F., Schachermayer, W. (1994). A general version of the fundamental theorem of asset pricing. Mathematische Annalen, Vol. 300, 463-520.

[Du96]   Duffie, D. (1996). Dynamic Asset Pricing Theory. 2nd Edition. Princeton University Press.

[EK99]   Elliott, R.J., Kopp, P.E. (1999). Mathematics of Financial Markets. Springer Finance, NY.

[Fe03]   Feldblum, S. (2003). Completing and using schedule P, Casualty Actuarial Society (CAS).

[FZ02]   Filipovic, D., Zabczyk, J. (2002). Markovian term structure models in discrete time. Ann. Applied Prob. 12/2, 710-729.

[FS04]   Föllmer, H., Schied, A. (2004). Stochastic Finance: An Introduction in Discrete Time. 2nd Edition. De Gruyter Studies in Mathematics 27, Berlin.

[GS94a]   Gerber, H.U., Shiu, E.S.W. (1994). Martingale approach to pricing perpetual American options. Proceedings of the 4th AFIR international colloquium, Orlando, April 20-22, 1994, 659-689.

[GS94b]   Gerber, H.U., Shiu, E.S.W. (1994). Option pricing by Esscher transforms. Transaction of Society of Actuaries 46, 99-140.

[Gi06]   Gisler, A. (2006). The estimation error in the chain-ladder reserving method: a Bayesian approach. ASTIN Bulletin 36/2, 554-565.

[IAA04]   IAA Insurer Solvency Assessment Working Party (2004). A global framework for insurer solvency assessment. International Actuarial Association IAA, Draft January 9, 2004.

[Ing87]   Ingersoll, J.E. (1987). Theory of Financial Decision Making. Rowman and Littlefield Publishers, Maryland.

[IAIS05]   International Association of Insurance Supervisors (IAIS). Glossary of terms, February 2005. Available under: http://www.iaisweb.org/

[Ja01]   Jarvis, S. (2001). Modern valuation techniques. Presented at the Staple Inn Actuarial Society, Feb. 6, 2001. Availble under http://www.sias.org.uk/papers/mvt.pdf

[LL91]   Lamberton, D., Lapeyre, B. (1991). Introduction au Calcul Stochastique appliqué à la Finance. Mathématiques et applications. SMAI no. 9, Ellipses-Edition.

[La04]   Landsman, Z. (2004). On the generalization of Esscher and variance premiums modified for the elliptical family of distributions. Insurance: Math. Econom. 35, 563-579.

[Ma93]   Mack, T. (1993). Distribution-free calculation of the standard error of chain ladder reserve estimates, ASTIN Bulletin 23/2, 213-225.

[MQB06]   Mack, T., Quarg, G., Braun, C. (2006). The mean square error of prediction in the chain ladder reserving method - a comment. ASTIN Bulletin 36/2, 543-552.

[MTW07]   Malamud, S., Trubowitz, E., Wüthrich, M.V. (2007). Market consistent pricing of insurance products. Preprint, ETH Zürich.

[Ma78]   Margrabe, W. (1978). The value of an option to exchange one asset for another. Journal of Finance 33/1, 177-186.

[Mi04]   Mikosch, T. (2004). Non-life Insurance Mathematics. An Introduction with Stochastic Processes. Unversitext, Springer, Berlin.

[Mu94]   Murphy, D.M. (1994). Unbiased loss development factors. Proc. CAS Vol. LXXXI, 154-222.

[Sa06]   Sandström, A. (2006). Solvency: Models, Assessment and Regulation. Chapman and Hall, CRC.

[Sa07]   Sandström, A. (2007). Solvency - an historical review and some pragmatic solutions. Bulletin SAA, 2007/1, 11-34.

[Sha02]   Sharma Report (2002). http://europa.eu.int/comm/internal_market/insurance/docs/solvency/solvency2-conference-report_en.pdf

[SW06]   Shevchenko, P.V., Wüthrich, M.V. (2006). Structural modelling of operational risk using Bayesian inference: Combining loss data with expert opinions. J. OpRisk 1/3, 3-26.

[SNB]   Statistisches Monatsheft der Schweizerischen Nationalbank SNB. Available under www.snb.ch

[SST06]   Swiss Solvency Test (2006). BPV SST Technisches Dokument, Version 2. October 2006. Available under www.bpv.admin.ch/themen/00506/00552

[Ta00]   Taylor, G. (2000). Loss Reserving: An Actuarial Perspective. Kluwer Academic Publishers.

[TA83]   Taylor, G.C., Ashe, F.R. (1983). Second moments of estimates of outstanding claims. J. Econometrics 23, 37-61.

[Ve90]   Verrall, R.J. (1990). Bayes and empirical Bayes estimation for the chain ladder model. ASTIN Bulletin 20, 217-243.

[Ve91]   Verrall, R.J. (1991). On the estimation of reserves from loglinear models. Insurance: Math. Econom. 10, 75-80.

[Wa02]   Wang, S. (2002). A set of new methods and tools for enterprise risk capital management and portfolio optimization. 2002 CAS Summer Forum, Dynamical Financial Analysis Discussion papers.

[Wü06a]   Wüthrich, M. (2006). Vom SST zu einem internen Risiko Management Tool für Nicht-Lebensversicherungen. In: Swiss Solvency Test, Eine Herausforderung auf vielen Ebenen, 30-34. J. Behrens and B. Locher (eds), Ernst & Young, Zürich, 2006.

[Wü06b]   Wüthrich, M. (2006). Premium liability risks: modeling small claims. Bulletin SAA, 2006/1, 27-38.

Index